SCRIPTURE-BASED DRAMAS

Finding God
in our daily lives

To the teenagers in my Sunday School class
for their enthusiasm in studying the Bible,
and the fun ways they inspired many of the characters
and storylines found in this book.

Scripture-based Dramas: Finding God in Our Daily Lives

© Rocky Neufeld, 2007

Library and Archives Canada Cataloguing in Publication

Neufeld, Rocky, 1961-
    Scripture-based dramas : finding God in our daily lives / Rocky Neufeld.

ISBN 978-1-894431-17-0

    1. Christian drama. 2. Drama in Christian education. I. Title.
II. Title: Finding God in our daily lives.

PN6120.R4N49 2007   808.82'9382   C2007-904756-4

Cover: © istockphoto.com/TriggerPhoto

Printed in Canada
October 2007

Your Nickel's Worth Publishing
Regina, SK.

www.yournickelsworth.com

TABLE OF CONTENTS

Christmas & Easter

BEATING THE CHRISTMAS BLUES
Isaiah 9:6-7

(Two friends meet, start to chat.)

JACK: Hi there, Joe—how're you doing?

JOE: You sure you really want to know?

JACK: What's that supposed to mean? Of course I want to know.

JOE: Well, it's just that it's December and Christmas will soon be here, and well...

JACK: Excuse me, I thought that was a good thing!

JOE: Don't get me wrong, I've got nothing against Christmas. It's just the before-Christmas part that makes me a little nuts.

JACK: But doesn't all that make Christmas even more meaningful when it does get here?

JOE: Who has time to think about the meaning of Christmas? At work it's our busiest time of year, so when I get home, I'm pretty much wiped right out, but then there's choir programs to practise for, Sunday School plays to rehearse, and—of course—all that money I have to spend on Christmas presents.

JACK: What do you mean you have to spend the money? It's not like someone is holding a gun to your head, forcing you to buy presents!

JOE: They might as well be. If I don't buy all my relatives just the right cool new clothes or the latest video games and equipment, it'll be a total disaster. And since that stuff is so expensive, there's no way I'll be able to buy myself that big-screen TV I've been looking at. I'll just have to give up stuff like that and ... I don't know, sometimes Christmas can be such a hassle.

JACK: So let me get this straight: you're upset because there's some inconvenience involved in Christmas and you have to make a bit of a sacrifice to make people you care about happy and spread the message of Christmas.

JOE: Well, I suppose that's true, although hearing you say it like that does make me seem a little selfish.

JACK: I'll say it does! What if Jesus had been worried about inconvenience or sacrifice? He probably would have never come to earth to be born a baby in a manger and given His life to save us from sin! I think it would be a good idea for you to remember that from now until Christmas—and beyond.

JOE: You're right. Compared to what Jesus put up with and endured on our behalf, I really have it pretty good.

JACK: Now you're starting to make some sense. Just remember, all the things we do for Christmas, they're to celebrate Jesus' birth. Thinking like that, you'll do all your Christmas preparations with a smile on your face.

JOE: You know, when I look at it that way, I might actually enjoy preparing for Christmas. And who needs a big screen TV? In our house I never get control of the remote anyway!

LEARNING FROM THE WISE MEN
Matthew 2:1-12

(Sunday School class is just over, KERI approaches the TEACHER.)

TEACHER: Hi, Keri.

KERI: Hey. I enjoyed class today, it was fun.

TEACHER: Thanks for your input. I really appreciate that you're always willing to say what you think, even if you don't always agree with what the teacher says. So, what's up? I have a feeling that you have more on your mind than just complimenting the Sunday School teacher.

KERI: You're right. I kind of have a problem and I need your advice. I told this guy I would get him my friend Stacy's phone number, but after I told him that I found out that he was really horrible to his last girlfriend. Now I feel like I better not give him her number. Is that the right thing to do?

TEACHER: Let me ask you this. What's the main reason you don't want to give your friend's phone number to this guy?

KERI: I don't want to see Stacy get hurt and from what I know about this guy there's a good chance he might hurt her.

TEACHER: Being guided by concern for your friend is a pretty good guideline in this situation. I would say you're doing exactly the right thing.

(TEACHER smiles, KERI notices.)

KERI: What?

TEACHER: What do you mean, "what"?

KERI: You just smiled. Did I do something dumb?
           What's so funny?

TEACHER: In Sunday School class you're always going
           on about how the Bible is full of
           entertaining stories but none of them have
           any meaning in today's world. Well, I
           think you just shot a bunch of holes in
           your own argument.

KERI: I don't get it. I never mentioned a Bible
           story.

TEACHER: True. But the situation you just described is
           quite similar to the story of the three wise
           men. They told King Herod they were
           searching for baby Jesus. Herod asked
           them to tell him as soon as they found
           Jesus, so Herod could come and worship
           him. The wise men agreed to this, but
           after they left, God showed them that
           Herod's real plan was to hurt Jesus. So,
           after the wise men found baby Jesus, they
           totally ignored Herod and took a different
           way home.

KERI: I get it ... so even though I told this guy I
           would give him Stacy's phone number,
           now that God has shown me he might
           hurt her, it's better if I don't help him get
           closer to her.

TEACHER: You catch on quick.

KERI: And I get your point, too. Not only is the
            Bible interesting to read, it can also help us
            with decisions we make every day. Thanks
            for the advice. See you. *(KERI moves to
            leave.)*

TEACHER: Thanks for listening. See you next Sunday.
            Remember, we'll be talking about what
            environmentalists can learn from the
            parting of the Red Sea.

IT'S BETTER TO GIVE
Luke 2:6-7

(Youth come in, TERRY throws coat down first, others throw theirs on top of it.)

TERRY: Christmastime is so much fun, especially when our Youth Group does stuff together. I'm really looking forward to Christmas caroling later. I wonder why we were told to meet here so early?

MAX: I have no idea. Our youth leaders love keeping us in suspense. So who's not here yet?

CHRIS: I don't see Darian. What's up with that, he's usually the first one here.

TERRY: I guess that means we've got some time to kill. So Chris, what do you want for Christmas?

CHRIS: I don't know, what do you want for Christmas?

(They go back and forth like this until MAX interrupts them.)

MAX: Would you two stop it already, that's really aggravating.

TERRY: Okay, we'll stop if you tell us what you want for Christmas.

MAX: Great. I hope I get a cell phone.

CHRIS: Oh, sure. That way you can talk on the phone all the time and ignore your friends who are actually there with you.

MAX: Well, if you're so smart, what do you want for Christmas?

CHRIS: I want a puppy. It'll be so much fun and, unlike a cell phone, my friends will have fun with it, too.

TERRY: But where you guys live, you have almost no yard. Dogs need room to run around and play. I think there should be some kind of law that you need to have a big yard or else you can't have a dog.

CHRIS: Since you seem to have all the answers, what do *you* want for Christmas?

TERRY: Oh, I just asked for money. That way no one can bug me about what I want for Christmas.

MAX: You are no fun at all.

(DARIAN enters, drops his coat with the others.)

CHRIS: Darian, you finally made it. What took you so long?

DARIAN: I was just talking to our youth pastor and you will not believe what he told me. Someone from our church, who didn't even leave their name, has given us $200! They just said it was a Christmas present for all of us and we have to use it as a group on something we can all agree on.

MAX: Adults think they're so smart, always trying to come up with ways to make us work together.

TERRY: I guess they must actually be smart then because we have to work together on an idea to spend this money.

CHRIS: I've got the perfect idea. We throw an awesome $200 Christmas party! We'll buy junk food, some cool new board games, rent movies and stay up all night, it'll be unforgettable! What do you guys think?

(Everyone in the group agrees until DARIAN speaks up.)

DARIAN: Guys, I have another idea of what we could do with the money.

CHRIS: No, Darian, whenever you have an idea it's sensible and I don't want to be sensible with this money.

MAX: We've got to be fair, you guys, everyone gets to have a say. Go ahead, Darian.

DARIAN: Thanks. I was just thinking about that new family at school. There's Joe and his sister and their parents. I talked to Joe the other day and they're having a tough time. Other than food, they don't have much money for anything else. Joe says they probably won't have any presents this Christmas or even a Christmas dinner. I think we should give the money to them.

CHRIS: What did I tell you, another sensible idea from Darian. *(Pauses to think.)* The party would have been awesome, but you're right, Darian. It's a much better idea to give the money to Joe and his family. What do you guys say?

(EVERYONE agrees.)

TERRY: I love this idea of helping their family out for Christmas. When I was a kid, adults kept telling me, "It's better to give than to receive." I never really knew what they meant until now. This'll be so much better than having a party.

MAX: I think it fits in real well with the Christmas story, too. God gave us the amazing gift of his son, little baby Jesus. I think it would make Jesus real happy that we're giving this gift to Joe and his family. And besides, Christmas is for everyone, not just people who go to our church.

DARIAN: So let's go tell them about their gift right now, they just live a few houses down the street here. Last one outside gets drilled with snowballs!

(They all rush to get their coats, TERRY is last, holds coat up like a shield on the way out.)

SCENE 2:

(JOE'S house, he's home alone reading a book, hears knock on door, lets youth group in.)

JOE: Come on in, guys! Boy is this ever a surprise!

DARIAN: Hi Joe. This is everyone from our Youth Group at our church just down the street.

JOE: Welcome here. So did you just drop by to introduce yourselves?

DARIAN: No, we've got a surprise for you. Actually, you could say it's a Christmas present. We just found out our group has been given $200 for Christmas. I told them how you're new in town and that you might not even have Christmas presents this year, so we all decided that we're going to tell our youth leaders to give you the money. Then you can do whatever you want with it.

JOE: This is unbelievable! Thank you, you guys are really amazing! If I was in your group, I would've probably just wanted to have a big all-night Christmas party with the money. But I'm not complaining. So why are you guys so unselfish?

MAX: We just felt like this is more in the spirit of Christmas and it's the type of thing Jesus would want us to do.

JOE: Well, thanks again. Just when I thought this was going to be the worst Christmas ever, now I think it's likely the *best* ever. You guys have such a cool group. If you don't mind my asking, what are you doing tonight?

CHRIS: We're going Christmas caroling. *(Looks at watch.)* And we need to get rolling and meet our youth leaders back at the church. Do you want to join us?

JOE: I'd love to. I'll just leave Mom and Dad a note so they know where I'm going. *(Scribbles on piece of paper.)*

DARIAN: By the way, Joe, I should warn you about this group. Seems like every time we're outside this time of year, someone starts a snowball fight. Isn't that right, Terry?

TERRY: Very funny. I'm warning you guys, I'm going to get all of you for what you did to me before.

DARIAN: Terry, I've seen you throw and I don't think we anything to worry about.

JOE: *(As JOE grabs his coat)* I guess I should warn you guys too then. At the school I went to before we moved here, I was the pitcher for our baseball team, and I love throwing snowballs almost as much as baseballs.

TERRY: *(Quickly moves next to JOE)* In that case, you're my new best buddy, Joe.

JOE: Let's go Christmas caroling.

(They all sing a carol as they exit together.)

CHRISTMAS DECORATIONS
1 John 4:9-11

DON: Look at all these amazing decorations—this must have taken a ton of work!

CHRIS: Yeah, it's all very impressive. But you know, *I* could do the decorating for something like this.

DON: That's a good one. You're so clumsy, your wife won't even let you use scissors anymore. How in the world would you make decorations for a banquet?

CHRIS: OK, so maybe indoor decorating isn't really my thing. But that reminds me, our yard is going to look sensational by the time Christmas gets here, if I do say so myself.

DON: Why, are you hiring someone to decorate it?

CHRIS: Nope, I'm doing it all by myself. I've still got some work to do, but it's coming along pretty well.

DON: And I see you've still got all your fingers. I guess that's what you call progress.

CHRIS: Very funny. You just wait 'til the yard is finished, then you won't be such a comedian.

DON: All right, I'll try to be serious. You realize that it's December, don't you? If this thing is gonna happen, you'd better get it done soon.

CHRIS: Relax, it'll be done in plenty of time. I do my best work under pressure.

DON: All right, so what's your yard going to look like when this mega-project is all done?

CHRIS: It's going to be a life-sized version of Santa and his sleigh and all of the reindeer on our roof, as if he just landed and is about to go down our chimney with a bunch of presents.

DON: That all sounds very nice, but I think you're forgetting one kind of important detail. I've been on your roof, in fact I helped you shingle it. There's no way you have enough room up there for all that stuff. If you want to have eight life-sized reindeer, Donner and Blitzen are going to fall off into your backyard.

(RICK comes in and listens to discussion without being noticed.)

CHRIS: Oh ye of little faith! I'll make it work somehow, even if the reindeer have to be a little smaller than life-size. But you have a lot of nerve criticizing my plans. I've seen your yard the last few years around Christmas and it looks like you're suffering from some extremely rare form of colour blindness that gets just a little worse each year.

DON: Like you know what you're talking about. No one has ever criticized my choice of colours.

CHRIS: That's probably because they remember how well you handle criticism. With you there's two sides to every argument, your side and the wrong side. So anyway, what have you got going on in *your* yard this year?

22

DON: It's the whole "Frosty the Snowman" theme. There's Frosty, of course, and some kids having a snowball fight with some glow in the dark snowballs to top it all off. I just have a couple more things to add and it'll be all ready for the public, and you, of course.

CHRIS: You sound pretty cocky. Next thing you know, you'll start charging admission. Of course mine will be done soon. too. It'd be done already if my kids would leave me alone. But they're always bugging me to drive them somewhere or, if they're at home, they want to help with the decorations. But I keep telling them, if they want to have the nicest yard on our street, they have to let me do it right.

DON: I know what you mean. Up 'til this year, if I didn't watch my kids every second, they'd grab my tools and start helping without me even asking them. But now I just find other things for them to do around the house to keep them distracted while I work on the decorations.

CHRIS: (Sees RICK) Oh hi, Rick, I didn't see you there. We need an unbiased opinion. Who has the better idea for yard decorations—me with Santa and his reindeer on the roof or Don with his sad attempt at "Frosty the Snowman."

RICK: I really don't care. In fact, I've probably never cared less about anything. You two are unbelievable. I heard you both talk about your decorations and how you don't let anyone help you. It's such a great opportunity to spend time with your kids, let them make something for your yard and feel good about it. Who cares if they do a less than professional job, this could be a great memory for them when they get older.

CHRIS: I don't know, Rick, you don't know what my kids are capable of. Both of them have done science projects this year for school and I'm still not sure what either of them were supposed to be.

DON: Really? I feel better now. I've seen stuff that my kids think is art but it looks more like something you'd see at a garbage dump.

RICK: You two are so busy competing with each other, you really don't get it. I just found out my sister has cancer. We hope she's going to be around for a long time, but I'm not taking any chances. If this is her last Christmas, I'm going to do my best to make it a memorable one.

In other words, I've got better things to do in the next few weeks than worry about whether my yard looks better than my neighbour's yard. Like the angels sang in the Christmas story, "Glory to God in the Highest, Peace on Earth Good Will to All." Spending meaningful time with family and friends, *that's* important. Well, I hope you guys will give this some thought. I've got to go. Merry Christmas. (*Rick leaves.*)

CHRIS: Amazing. Rick just got this bad news about his sister and he can still make fun of you—he's such a cool guy.

DON: Wait a minute. He was making fun of you, too.

CHRIS: I know, I know. I was just seeing if you were paying attention. But what he says makes a lot of sense. This weekend I'm going to ask my kids how they want to finish decorating the yard, and then help them do it.

DON: Amen to that. Our yard probably won't end up looking the way I thought it would, but if the kids help it'll be even better. Merry Christmas.

CHRIS: Merry Christmas, Don. *(They both exit.)*

WHAT IS EASTER?
Luke 24:6-7

(Two teenagers meet after school.)

DYLAN: Hey, what's up?

ALEX: Not much, but I'm sure looking forward to the long weekend.

DYLAN: I hear ya, the teachers have been working us far too hard lately.

ALEX: The extra day off school is nice, but I was just thinking, Easter is kind of a lame holiday.

DYLAN: Oh really, Einstein. I've known you for a long time and I always figured the most you think about anything is deciding when to fall asleep in history class. But this took a bit of pondering. So what've you got against Easter?

ALEX: Well, with Easter, you've got the Easter Bunny, and kids looking for Easter eggs, and that's pretty much it. Now you look at Christmas— there's an awesome holiday. You've got your Santa Claus and of course he's bringing awesome Christmas presents, and then there's extremely fun Christmas parties going on everywhere you look. It's just a great holiday.

DYLAN: Wait a minute, is this all you know about Christmas and Easter?

ALEX: Yeah, why? Are there secrets that somebody's been keeping from me?

DYLAN: This is amazing! I've heard people say our education system is messed up and now I think I know what they mean! It's time I gave you some truth.

Christmas celebrates the birth of God's son, Jesus Christ, here on earth, and the reason we have Easter is because Jesus died and then rose from the dead two days later. He did all that to save us from our sins, because I don't know if you've realized it or not, but people can get pretty messed up sometimes. So Jesus died for our sins so that we wouldn't have to, and now through Him we can all have eternal life.

ALEX: Wow! That sounds like some of those super hero movies I love watching.

DYLAN: But with Jesus, it's a lot better. He loves everybody, not just heroes with super powers. And no matter how much you like a movie, it's always over in a couple of hours or so, but Jesus is always there, whenever you need him.

ALEX: Wait a minute. We go to the same school, take the same classes, how come you know about this stuff and I don't?

DYLAN: While you sleep in on Sunday mornings, my parents have always taken me to church. When I was younger, I kind of thought it was boring, but back then I was pretty lame. Now I'm so glad I've learned about Jesus. It's like He goes with me everywhere.

ALEX: What do you mean? I just see you, same as always. Is He like your invisible friend?

DYLAN: I guess that's one way of looking at it. Jesus lives inside of me and helps me be a better person.

ALEX: Cool. But you're still always ready to give me a hard time about not being as smart as you. I totally got that Einstein crack, you know. Doesn't stuff like that get you in trouble with Jesus?

DYLAN: Relax, I was just having some fun. That's one of God's creations, too.

ALEX: Since He created it, we might as well make the most of it. Let's see what's going on in the school gym. And I'm sure I'll think of some more questions for you about Christmas and Easter too.

DYLAN: Deal. Let's go.

(They both exit.)

Church

USING OUR GIFTS
Romans 12:5-8

(JOE reads scripture for church service, CAREY approaches him afterward.)

CAREY: You did a really good job reading scripture today, reading very expressively and looking up at the congregation a lot.

JOE: Are you sure? I was scared you would say it was kind of weak and pathetic.

CAREY: Oh no, I thought it was excellent. But next time you do it, if you read just a bit slower it could be even better.

JOE: Thanks for the advice. I'll definitely try to do that next time.

CAREY: Uh, Joe could I talk to you about something?

JOE: Sure, what's on your mind?

CAREY: Well, you have a gift for reading scripture. There are so many other gifted people in our church, whether it's singing in the choir or leading meetings or teaching Sunday School or whatever. There just doesn't seem to be anything that I'm good at.

JOE: You're kidding right? What did you just say to me?

CAREY: Uh, "Joe could I talk to you about something?"

JOE: No, no, I mean before that.

CAREY: You mean about your good work at reading scripture?

JOE: Exactly. You told me I had done a good job and then you helped me try to do it better.

CAREY: So what? What's so great about that?

JOE: You have the gift of encouragement. I was thinking about quitting scripture reading because I didn't think I was any good at it. But you've shown me otherwise and because of that I think I'll keep doing it. And I've seen you do the same thing with other people. You have a real knack for helping people get the best out of their gifts. So don't let me ever again hear you talking this crap about not having any gifts, OK?

CAREY: OK, OK, I get the message. Thanks Joe, it's so nice to know that I have something I can contribute to our church. I feel like encouraging someone else. Where is our pastor? I'm going to go find him and tell him how good his sermons have been lately—and I have this great idea how they could be even better. See you soon.

(CAREY exits.)

THINK POSITIVE
Luke 6:38

(JOE and RUTH are discussing church finances.)

JOE: Hello there, how are you doing?

RUTH: Oh, I'm all right.

JOE: So did you hear about what came out of the last church council meeting? I guess we're way behind where we should be for offerings at this time of year.

RUTH: I know. With Christmas on the way, we should be focusing on the coming of the little baby Jesus. But instead, we're having all this talk about money. I just don't like this whole negative atmosphere.

JOE: I realize it's unpleasant to hear about things we may lose if we don't increase our giving, but how else can we effectively get the message across?

RUTH: Well, I think we could focus on all the positive things we can do if everyone finds a way to give a bit more. For instance, our church building has long been in need of some work in a few spots. Most of us put a lot of time and money into looking after our own homes, it would be great to do the same for God's house.

JOE: Wow. I never thought of it that way. I guess you can teach an old dog like me some new tricks. It would be wonderful if we could increase our giving enough to take care of all the work that needs to be done on this building.

RUTH: I'm so glad you agree. Now let's go tell everyone else in the church and get them excited about it, too.

(They exit.)

WHEN IT'S GOOD TO BE SELFISH
Luke 6:46-49

(RICK is reading, TERRY walks in.)

TERRY: Hey Rick, what'cha working at there?

RICK: Oh hi, Terry, I'm just getting ready for teaching Sunday School today.

TERRY: That's interesting, because it's kind of related to what I wanted to talk to you about.

RICK: OK, I know last-minute studying like this isn't considered the greatest preparation method, but I seem to get my best ideas when there's a bit of pressure on me.

TERRY: Relax, I'm not here to criticize how you get yourself ready to teach.

RICK: *(Puts book down.)* In that case, you have my undivided attention and I think I'm ready for class anyway. What's up?

TERRY: Well, you know that our church has started regular small group meetings, right?

RICK: Yeah, sure. So how has that been going?

TERRY: Pretty well. Of course *our* group is the coolest group. *(Smiles.)* But I wanted to ask you, have you been going to any of the small groups?

RICK: No, I haven't. With teaching Sunday School and working with the youth group and singing in the choir and all the other stuff, my schedule is pretty full.

TERRY: Now don't get me wrong, all those activities are tremendously important and your involvement is greatly appreciate by everyone in the church. But in those things you mentioned, you are mainly providing spiritual nourishment to others. I really think it would do you good to be more selfish sometimes.

RICK: OK, I can be selfish. *(Pauses to think.)* You probably noticed my car is filthy, and I have been feeling pretty tired lately what with my busy schedule. So could you wash it for me in the next day or two?

TERRY: Very funny. That's not what I meant. I'm talking about being more selfish when it comes to your own spiritual nourishment. Instead of having to lead the discussion like you do as a Sunday School teacher, in our small group someone else leads. Being in such a group, you can learn a lot just listening to the spiritual views and ideas of other believers.

I know I sure have, whether it's discussing a Bible passage or a book written by a contemporary Christian author. And we always allow time to pray for everyone's prayer requests. Just knowing I have the complete support of others in our group is a tremendous blessing. That's what I mean by looking after your own spiritual nourishment.

RICK: So I guess washing my car is definitely out then.

TERRY: Yeah. Definitely.

RICK: *(Smiles.)* Sorry, just couldn't resist. But I *am* going to start coming to your small group. Even though I'm pretty busy, you've made me realize that I need to make time for something this important. *(Looks at his watch.)* But right now it's time for Sunday School. See you at small group.

TERRY: Sounds great!

(They both exit.)

CONFLICT, A HEALTHY PART OF LIFE
Acts 2:42-47

(BRUCE and DENNIS sit talking.)

BRUCE: Well, Dennis, I thought the series we just finished in our small group was quite thought-provoking.

DENNIS: I agree, and it gave me an idea for what we could discuss next. We could look at witnessing, and talking to strangers about Jesus.

BRUCE: There's no doubt witnessing is extremely important. But how much impact do our words have if the other person doesn't know us?

DENNIS: So what do you suggest, we just walk right by strangers and ignore them instead of telling them about Jesus?

BRUCE: Not at all. What I'm saying is that I think we should first get to know them, show we're interested in them.

DENNIS: I disagree. They need to know right away what's most important in our lives. The first thing we say to them should be about our relationship with Jesus.

BRUCE: What? You might as well just carry a sledgehammer and hit them over the head with it! They'll likely accuse you of thinking you're better than they are—or they might just totally ignore you.

DENNIS: At least I'm willing to put forth the effort. It sounds like you're just looking for their approval, trying to be more like the world. Well, I figure with Jesus on my side, I have no need to fear being different. I put my faith in Jesus that He'll win over their souls once I tell them that I'm a born-again Christian and how great it is.

BRUCE: Wait a minute, what are we arguing about? Who says we all have to take exactly the same approach to witnessing?

DENNIS: You're right. If you truly believe you're doing the Lord's work, that's the main thing.

BRUCE: You know what, this could be a fascinating way to discuss witnessing in our small group.

DENNIS: You mean, the sledgehammer approach to witnessing? *(Big smile.)*

BRUCE: That was kind of a stupid thing to say. I apologize, I need to think before shooting my mouth off like that.

DENNIS: Don't worry about it, stuff like that keeps me on my toes. And besides, I apologize too; I never should have made that crack about your approach being too worldly. But I see what you mean about our small group. We could discuss different approaches to witnessing and really help everyone think about how they can best spread the Word of the Lord.

BRUCE: Amen to that. But I'm kind of glad we had this little difference of opinion. I think it'll be quite helpful in the long run. Let's go tell the rest of the group. *(They exit.)*

PRIORITIES
Acts 20:35

(TEACHER and KASEY have a chat after class.)

TEACHER: So how did you like Sunday School class?

KASEY: It was pretty cool having so many kids today, it was a lot of fun.

TEACHER: Yeah, I think 12 is a new record for our Senior Youth class. I just hope everyone keeps coming back.

KASEY: Oh, I'm sure at least most of them will.

TEACHER: I wish I had your faith. I don't know if I should tell you this but I guess you'll find out eventually. Our youth pastor is only going to be with us for a couple more months and then we'll have to let him go.

KASEY: What? But we waited so long to have a youth pastor and we're having such a good time with him. He makes it so much fun to read the Bible and talk about our Christian faith. Why would the church just kick him out?

TEACHER: Money. Giving is down, expenses are up. Bottom line is we can't afford a youth pastor any more.

KASEY: But can't they find another way to save money?

TEACHER: We've cut everything back as much as we can already. I'm sorry, I wish there was another way.

KASEY: You and me both. You know, I was thinking of becoming a church member some day but now I don't think I want to anymore. I mean, why join a church where people don't even care enough to give enough offering to have a youth pastor.

(KASEY walks out, TEACHER watches then exits also.)

SUNDAY SCHOOL MEMORIES
Psalms 145:8-13

(Mr. Jacobs is preparing for Sunday School. Former student Dan walks in.)

DAN: Mind if I come in for a minute?

MR. JACOBS: Well, hello there, Dan! Come on in. Boy it's been a long time since I've seen you—I guess ever since you moved away. How are you doing? What brings you back?

DAN: I'm doing super! I'm just back in town for my cousin's wedding, so I thought it would be a good time to come in and say hello.

MR. JACOBS: I'm glad you did. As you can see, I'm just getting ready for another Sunday School class. I still enjoy it, but it's been a long time since we've had a character in this class as colourful as you were.

DAN: That's an awfully nice way of saying I was a troublemaker.

MR. JACOBS: I prefer to think of it as you keeping me on my toes. Let's see if I remember some of the creative ideas you came up with: stealing my chalk, sticking used bubblegum on the seat of my chair so I ended up sitting on it—and my personal favourite—tying my shoelaces together one time when I was sitting in my chair trying to explain something to the class. It was nice to know I could make everyone laugh, falling on my face like that.

DAN: I'm just grateful that you didn't give up on me and kick me out of the class for good.

MR. JACOBS: Oh no, I never would have done that. Although I will admit one thing. You see this gray hair on my head? It's not the result of a clever dye job. I'm pretty sure you caused a lot of it. But I wouldn't have it any other way. *(Pause)*

Since you're here, I need to ask your honest opinion about something. Lately I've been wondering if I'm doing any good here any more. Sometimes I get the idea that kids pay attention real well while they're in this class but they don't seem to get any use from what we study when they get into the outside world. What do you think?

DAN: I can only tell you my own experience. When I started coming here I had a bad attitude, mostly because my parents made me come. That's probably why I pulled a lot of those dumb pranks. At that time there were a lot of chances for me to get into the wrong crowd with kids my age who were doing drugs and other stupid things, and sometimes ending up in jail. But you kept working on me, and eventually it started to make sense.

Becoming a follower of Jesus changed my whole life. Instead of being selfish like the kids in my old neighbourhood, I started looking for ways to help others and spread God's love. A lot of that came directly from what you taught in this class. So, I'm sorry about causing your gray hair, but I think it was worth it in the long run.

MR. JACOBS: I'll say it was! Wow! That's really great to hear. It's wonderful that you got something useful out of coming to Sunday School.

DAN: I sure did—and here's another thing that you may find interesting. For the last few years I've been teaching Sunday School, just like you. I've realized that even though I sometimes don't feel like I know what I'm doing, it does seem to make a difference in their lives.

MR. JACOBS: And again I say, wow! It never occurred to me that someone I taught would end up being called to do the same thing with other kids. So why did you decide to start?

DAN: Mostly because you helped me realize how great it is to be a born-again Christian, and I wanted to try and do the same thing for other kids.

MR. JACOBS: Thanks for sharing this with me, Dan—and keep up the good work.

DAN: I'll do my best. But you know what? Sometimes when I come up against a really difficult challenge, all I do is try to figure out what you would have done in that same situation and it usually works. So thanks again for being my favourite Sunday School teacher, and keep doing it.

MR. JACOBS: After what you've just told me, I'm looking forward to it even more.

(Dan leaves, Mr. Jacobs continues studying.)

DOING GOD'S WORK
Ephesians 2:11-16

(Middle-aged MR. DAVIS sits alone, looking depressed. Younger DARRYL walks in.)

RYAN: Hello, Mr. Davis. Do you mind if I join you?

MR. DAVIS: Not at all, have a seat.

RYAN: Thanks. I couldn't help but notice— you're looking kind of low. What's up?

MR. DAVIS: Are you sure you want to hear about my problems?

RYAN: Hey, you've listened to me rant plenty of times about the stuff that gets on *my* nerves. It's about time I did the same for you.

MR. DAVIS: Thanks, maybe it'll help to talk about this. The thing is, lately I've just had this overwhelming feeling that I've never done anything important in terms of spreading the love of Jesus. I don't know if it's a mid-life crisis, but it just feels like there's this big wall in front of me that I'll never get over.

RYAN: I'm sure glad you told me about this. You think you have this wall in front of you but you really don't.

MR. DAVIS: I appreciate your optimism but how could you possibly know that?

RYAN: Well, I'll tell you a story that my dad told me. Do you remember back when my family first moved here and my dad came to work for the same company where you were working at the time?

MR. DAVIS: Sure, he looked very unsure of himself at first, but it didn't take him long to get over that.

RYAN: That's right. And he's told me many times how much he appreciated your help with that. You introduced yourself the very first day and helped him find his way around the office. Then you invited our whole family to church, and the first Sunday we came, you made us all feel welcome.

My parents eventually made some great friends in this church and we've been coming to worship here regularly ever since. Seeing that my parents were happy here, I've also become involved in this church and expect to be coming here for a long time. And all this happened because you went out of your way to be a friend to my dad and to show him the love of Jesus.

MR. DAVIS: I don't know what to say. Are you sure all that is because of me?

RYAN: I know it is. Just think, if it wasn't for you, our family may have given up on church. Who knows, I might have joined a street gang and become a bank robber or a drug dealer. So you see, you *have* done incredibly important work in spreading the love of Jesus. You made it possible for me to develop a personal relationship with Him. That wall you were talking about before? It's gone, blown to pieces.

MR. DAVIS: Thanks, Ryan. I really appreciate you telling me this, it makes me feel so much better. You sure have changed a lot from the bratty kid who used to make so much noise in church when we were all trying to listen to the sermon.

RYAN: I was really hoping everyone had forgotten about that by now. I guess I need to make up for lost time. Let's go, the sermon's about to start.

MR. DAVIS: Lead the way, I'm right behind you.

(They both exit.)

FORGIVENESS IS THE LORD'S DOING
Revelation 4:1-8

(Two long-time adult friends meet CENTRE STAGE and talk.)

LARRY: *(Depressed. Sighs.)* Hi, Jerry.

JERRY: *(Energetic.)* Hey, Larry, How's it going?

LARRY: *(Pauses, scratches his head.)* You sure you wanna know?

JERRY: Of course I do. Why, is there something wrong?

LARRY: I'll see if I can explain it. You know that I was saved a long time ago and that I'm a regular church-goer. But lately I guess I've developed more self-awareness, and I realize now that I'm a pretty big jerk.

JERRY: Listen, I know I call you a jerk sometimes but that's because we're friends. It's all in fun, I don't mean anything by it.

LARRY: That's not the problem. You're one of my best friends and I know you like to joke around like that. Just like when I call you a pinhead with no fashion sense. It's all for fun. My problem is much worse than that. Where should I start?

I have a problem with envy. When people accomplish something important, I'm never happy for them. I'm always thinking that they're just lucky, that they don't deserve their success, and I find myself wishing that something bad would happen to them and their success would be taken away. And I'm always being critical of people. If someone does something special for the church service, I never stop until I find a flaw in what they did that I can criticize. Even if it's the slightest little stumble during a scripture reading. What do I do?

JERRY: Well, if you really want to change, I think you need to pray about it. Tell God what you just told me and ask His forgiveness. And then really work at it but be patient. Take things one step at a time.

LARRY: Do you really think God would forgive me? I remember reading in Revelation, where it talks about heaven and thrones and precious metals and golden crowns. God is so almighty and powerful, why would He want to forgive a petty little sinner like me?

JERRY: You're right about God being almighty and all powerful, but there's something else about Him you need to remember. In a way, His love is wonderfully simple. His forgiveness is available to everyone who asks. He loves everybody, including murderers, robbers and petty little jerks like you *(pauses and smiles)*—just kidding.

LARRY: *(Smiles.)* Thanks for listening to me rant. What you say makes a lot of sense.

JERRY: But remember, take things slow. For example, from now on when people read scripture in church, make a point of ignoring any little mistakes and find a way to give them a compliment. If it was me, you could congratulate me on my tremendous fashion sense.

LARRY: I don't know about that, I think it'd be easier for me to set a world record in the 100 metre dash. I'm just playing, that sounds like a great plan. Thanks again.

JERRY: Not a problem. Listen, I'm going over to the church to help with the annual cleaning day. Do you want to pitch in?

LARRY: Why should I help? I'm not the one who messed up the Sunday School rooms and tracked mud all over the place. Let someone else— *(pauses, looks at JERRY.)* Wait a minute, I'm trying to stop being negative and critical all the time. *(Takes a deep breath.)* I would love to help with church cleaning. Let's go.

(They both exit.)

(DON is sitting, preparing to teach Sunday School. Friend CAREY walks in.)

CAREY: Hi Don, could I talk to you for a minute?

DON: Oh, hi. *(Looks at his watch.)* Sure, Sunday School doesn't start for a few minutes yet, have a seat. What's on your mind?

CAREY: I just wanted to say that I and a lot of other people in our church really appreciate that you've been able to take over teaching one of our Sunday School classes. How's it been going so far?

DON: I've really enjoyed it. Of course, I was scared to death before the first class, but it has been a great experience for me and I've learned a lot. It's really amazing, because it wasn't very long ago that I had no time for Sunday School or any other kind of volunteering.

CAREY: Well, we're lucky that you have time now. So what happened?

DON: The big turning point was when we decided to sell our farm. In the past I was always so determined to have a successful farm, but a series of poor crops and low grain prices were just too much to overcome. Instead of waiting for the bank to tell us we had to get out, we decided to just sell instead.

cont'd ...

But after we made that decision, I reached probably the lowest point of my life. I felt like I was failing my whole family, since the farm has been in our family for three generations. It hurt so bad and I really didn't know what to do.

CAREY: That sounds awful, yet you look so happy now. What changed?

DON: Just when I was feeling really sorry for myself, my neighbour called. His hired man had just quit and he really need someone to take over who had some farming experience, or at least someone who knew the difference between wheat and walnuts. I couldn't think of anyone, but told him I'd let him know if I did. After I hung up the phone it suddenly occurred to me, as though God had turned on this thousand-watt light bulb in my brain, that I could be my neighbour's new hired man. So I called him back and I've been working for him ever since. It's been great.

CAREY: That's wonderful, but what made you decide to start teaching Sunday School?

DON: Now that my responsibility is just to look after the farm work, all the pressure I felt in the past is gone. I no longer spend every waking hour worrying about the farm, going over the books, trying to find some way to create profit. Some people enjoy the management end of farming, but I just wasn't one of them. So, with some spare time on my hands, I decided to get involved with Sunday School. God has lifted me up and opened my eyes and I'm so much happier working with the kids in my class, instead of always worrying about the farm the way I did in the past.

CAREY: Isn't it amazing how God always seems to know what's best for us even when we might not have a clue?

DON: I'm living proof of that. You know, It's great that you appreciate me teaching Sunday School, but I'm just so grateful for the opportunity. Just being aware of all that God has done for me and having more time to enjoy life is really amazing.

CAREY: I see your joy rubbing off on the kids in your class.

DON: Thanks, that's good to know. *(Looks at his watch.)* Speaking of Sunday School, I think the kids are going to be here any second. I don't know how to tell you this, but I think we're going to need that chair.

CAREY: Say no more. I'll talk to you later, keep up the good work!

(CAREY exits, DON turns his attention back to his preparations.)

Family

THE PRODIGAL
Luke 15:11-32

(DAD and TERI walk in from opposite sides, he looks happy, she looks sad.)

TERI: Hi, Dad.

DAD: Teri, it is so good to see you. *(Moves to greet her.)* Welcome home! Why do you look so sad?

TERI: Dad I need to tell you something—and then you probably won't be so happy to see me.

DAD: Is it that you never really went to that university on the other side of the country last fall, after telling us that's what you were going to do?

TERI: How did you know that?

DAD: Well, your Mom and I called the university a few weeks ago. We want to meet your instructors to see what they were like, but they had no record of you being there.

TERI: So why didn't you call me and yell at me when you found out?

DAD: You're a big girl now. We wanted to let you work things out for yourself.

TERI: OK, you know that part, but it gets worse. The money you gave me for school, well, it's all gone. I've been having a real good time with my friends, but having fun is expensive. Dad, I'm so sorry. Can you forgive me?

DAD: Of course I forgive you. I'm your Dad. It's part of the job description.

TERI: Thanks, that means a lot to me. I promise I will make it up to you. I'll get a job and pay you back, every penny.

DAD: Hey, wait a minute. That was your money, we've always planned that you would have it. So if anything, you need to pay yourself back.

TERI: It's a deal, and then I'll go back to school and get my education. *(Steels herself.)* OK, Dad, I'm ready as I'll ever be.

DAD: *(Acts like he has no idea what she means)* Ready? Ready for what? Oh, you must mean dinner. Yeah, it sure smells good, your Mom is going all out today.

TERI: Not that, although it really does smell good. I mean I'm ready for my punishment for wasting all that money. I'm sure you've got a real good one planned for me.

DAD: I think going through this whole ordeal has punished you enough—and I think you've also learned a valuable lesson because you're already taking responsibility for your actions. I'm just thrilled that you actually came home and confided in me. For a while, your Mom and I have felt like we weren't really a part of your life any more. It's so great to have you back!

TERI: Wow! I really don't deserve this!

DAD: Well, we think you do. And besides, Jesus forgives all our sins; me, you, your Mom— everyone. So, all I'm trying to do is follow His example.

TERI: You know, I never really understood what Jesus has to offer me, but thanks to you, I think I'm starting to get it.

DAD: Hey, just another part of the Dad's job description. But Dads also need to eat, and so do daughters.

TERI: Sounds awesome. Let's go.

(They exit together.)

PEACE IT TOGETHER
Luke 18:1-8

(DYLAN is reading a history book, he looks up as DAD enters)

DYLAN: Hey, Dad, what's up?

DAD: Not much, Dylan, what are you working at?

DYLAN: Oh, I'm just doing some homework. Remember how I told you a while back how school is so boring and we never learn anything interesting?

DAD: I remember it well. I believe your exact words were, "I thought teachers were supposed to be so smart. How can they be smart and be so incredibly dull at the same time?"

DYLAN: Yeah, I guess I was a little harsh. I think I'm starting to change my mind. We're learning about World War II and it is really interesting!

DAD: Is that right? What exactly is it that's got you so fascinated?

DYLAN: Well, the Germans started out all tough and basically ran over France and some other countries. Then they were beating the daylights out of England for a while, but the British really hung in there and eventually—with the help of the Americans and us Canadians—our side won the war. It's really amazing!

DAD: It's a nice story when you put it that way, but I think you're missing something very important. There was a lot of death and suffering. It's estimated that over 16 million people died in that war, including nearly 40,000 Canadians. So I think it's great that you're learning about the war, but you should also realized that it was a horrible time for a lot of people.

DYLAN: OK, I guess you've got a point. But a lot of those deaths were our enemies, so they probably deserved it.

DAD: Wait a minute, that's a pretty big assumption. And even if they were on Hitler's side, does that make it right to kill them? I suppose it's natural to want revenge. But remember that we're Mennonites and we believe in pacifism. Jesus told us it's easy to be nice to people who are friends with us. His challenge for us was to love those who treat us badly.

DYLAN: So are you talking about during the war, or right now today?

DAD: I don't think Jesus had any time limits, so I think it means for always. And another thing I always like to remind myself: the commandment says 'Thou shalt not kill.' It does not say, 'Thou shalt not kill except if they're real jerks or on the wrong side, then it's OK to blow them away.' Am I making any sense?

DYLAN: Yeah, I guess you are. It's kind of like at school, there's this girl in some of my classes and we always seem to be on the opposite side of every debate. Instead of hating her guts for disagreeing with me, I kind of admire her for standing up for her beliefs and for challenging me to really think about what *I* believe.

DAD: Wow. I am really proud of you. Whoever said that today's teenagers are all selfish and just think about themselves all the time obviously didn't know what they were talking about. It's like you're taking the words of Jesus and putting them into action.

DYLAN: Thanks, Dad. Since you are so proud of me, how about buying me that new video game that I want so bad.

DAD: There he is, our typical normal teenager. Tell you what, you get your marks out from under water below 'C' level to where they should be and we'll talk about that video game.

DYLAN: OK, it's a deal. Now leave me alone so I can do some more studying.

DAD: See you later, son.

(DAD walks out, Dylan continues reading.)

PEACE IN OUR TIME
Ephesians 2:11-14

(Dad is reading, Jessica comes in. Dad looks up.)

DAD: Hi Jess, how was school today?

JESSICA: Oh, the same old boring crap from hundred-year-old text books. I wish that in just one of our classes we could learn about something that actually happened in the last ten years.

DAD: Well, why don't you make that into your own little project—you could become a famous writer of modern history.

JESSICA: That would be pretty cool, but then I would have to hire someone to do my homework. It's unbelievable how they keep piling it on!

DAD: Maybe you can write that book when you get older. Listen, I wanted to ask you, did you do like I asked and get things straightened out with the friend you had a fight with? What was her name, Kathy, Katy, Karey?

JESSICA: You know, Dad, I hope I never get as old as you. You can't remember anything. Her name is Cassidy.

DAD: Well at least give me credit for being close. Speaking of forgetting stuff, what was that fight about anyway?

JESSICA: Like I told you before, we were in a drama for church. It started out good, but we got all mixed up about halfway through and it turned out awful. Cassidy said it was all my fault and, of course, I accused her of causing all the trouble. But we're past all that now.

DAD: I'm glad to hear you worked things out. Was it a hard thing to do?

JESSICA: Not really. We just got together and talked, and realized that it didn't really matter whose fault it was. The bottom line is that the drama bombed. We both want to get involved and do a better job the next time there's a drama at church. After all, it's God's house and He deserves our best.

DAD: I've got to tell you, I'm really proud of you and the way you handled that situation. A lot of grown-ups aren't mature enough to resolve a conflict the way you and your friend did.

JESSICA: Thanks, Dad. *(pause)* I was just thinking, this is kind of the same as your situation with Mr. Davis. You know, about what happened in church a couple of weeks ago when you both were singing in the male quartet?

DAD: I don't think it's the same at all. He's been behaving like a complete lunatic, accusing me of starting the song too low just so I could show off how low I can sing. The nerve of that guy.

JESSICA: Dad, you're behaving like a five-year-old kid.

DAD: Am not.

JESSICA: Are too.

DAD: Am not. *(Stops suddenly and smiles)* OK, maybe I am just a bit. So, since you're the one with all the wisdom when it comes to conflict resolution, what do you think I should do?

JESSICA: That's better. Maybe there's hope that you still might grow up and act like a mature adult some day. What you and Mr. Davis should do is just sit down and talk about it. I think you should forget about what happened before and start thinking about the next time the quartet sings in church.

And just to be on the safe side, you should have someone play piano for you next time, so no one can be accused of starting too low or too high or whatever. Just concentrate on praising God through your music.

DAD: That actually could work. So where did you get all this common sense from?

JESSICA: Obviously not from you. But don't worry, Dad, I'm always available to listen to your problems. Right now though, I need you for your scientific knowledge. Do you think you could help me with my homework?

DAD: It would be my pleasure, and it's kind of reassuring that you don't know everything about everything—at least not yet. Let's go.

(They exit.)

MOTHERS JUST KNOW
Ephesians 6:1

(DAD is looking around, kind of out of it, son or daughter MAX walks in.)

MAX: Hey, Dad—what's up? You look kind of lost. Did you forget where you put the remote for the TV again?

DAD: Good one. So are you just here to torment your semi-forgetful old dad, or do you really want to know what's on my mind?

MAX: Dad, I was just kidding. Of course I want to know what you're thinking about.

DAD: Well, even though your Grandma died nearly a year ago, I really miss her today, probably because it's Mother's Day.

MAX: Yeah, I miss her too, and not just because she was my Grandma. She was really cool.

DAD: I never thought of her that way, but you're right, she was highly cool. I remember one time back when our family still lived on the farm. I was about your age and this one day it was at least a thousand degrees outside. I was cleaning out a steel granary and of course it was even hotter in there. I was ticked off at your Grandpa for making me do that sweaty, stinky job. All of a sudden your Grandma was at the grain bin door with a glass of iced tea. It was like she knew exactly when I was the most frustrated and tired, and that's when she showed up . I still remember how good that iced tea tasted.

MAX: That's awesome! Did you ever tell her how much you appreciated stuff like that?

DAD: I told her I loved her quite often. I don't know, maybe I should have said more.

MAX: I'm sure she knew how much she meant to you. Somehow moms just know. (MAX *pauses and thinks.*) Mom's a lot like that. I never thought of this before, but sometimes she just knows what I need even before I do. One time I was in my room doing math homework that I really didn't understand, and that same day I'd had a major fight with my best friend. I was already frustrated about the fight and the homework was just making it worse. It seemed like the worst day ever. Suddenly Mom knocked on my door and said she just wanted to talk. I have no idea how she did it, but she knew exactly how I was feeling. I don't remember what we talked about, but when she left a few minutes later, suddenly I wasn't having such a bad day any more.

DAD: That doesn't surprise me. We sure are lucky to have her. I hope she liked the Mother's Day present we gave her.

MAX: I'm going to go find her right now and tell her how great she is. God sure knew what he was doing when he created mothers. Where is Mom anyway?

DAD: I don't know, probably doing something nice for us. Can I come along?

MAX: Sure, but let me do the talking OK? You're not exactly Mr. Smooth when it comes to saying nice things to people.

DAD: All right, you're the boss. I'll be quiet. *(They head toward the door.)* I think she's going to like this better than any present we could give her.

(They exit.)

PRACTISING JUSTICE & MERCY

1 Timothy 5:1-8, 17-24

(DAD is sitting at table, Mike walks in.)

MIKE: Hey, Dad.

DAD: Hi, Mike. So how was Sunday School class today?

MIKE: It was actually pretty interesting. We talked about practising justice and mercy, and how it says in the Bible we're supposed to look after widows, poor people and others that are having a hard time.

But it got me thinking, that should also apply to those of us who mess up. Sure, you need to have the justice—jail time or fines or in my case almost non-stop groundings. But after we've done our time, we need to be treated with mercy and given a chance to be productive people, the same as those who don't make any major mistakes.

DAD: You've obviously given this a lot of thought; I'm impressed.

MIKE: Thanks. So, you excited about my basketball game tomorrow night? I know I am.

DAD: Sure, the game. *(Gasps)* Oh no, I completely forgot and now I've volunteered to work tomorrow night and I can't get out of it. I'm so sorry.

MIKE: Unbelievable! You always do this. You tell me you'll be there to see me play a game or whatever and then you forget or back out. And you say I've got a problem with being irresponsible?

DAD: Now, don't forget what you've learned about being merciful ...

MIKE: That's only half of it, you also need to have justice.

DAD: You know, you're right. It's pretty stupid of me to tell you to do one thing and go off and do the opposite myself. I've got an idea. When you do something stupid or irresponsible, you get punished, right?

(Mike nods.)

Forgetting about your game was pretty irresponsible of me, so I should be punished. I guess it's up to you to decide my punishment.

MIKE: Now *this* I can get into! You know, Dad, normally your attempts to distract me from being mad at you are pretty weak and pathetic, but this one might actually have some merit. *(Mike pauses, thinks over options.)* OK, here's your punishment. For the next two weeks you are in charge of cleaning up my room, including making my bed. So if Mom starts yelling about my messy room like she often does, she'll be yelling at you.

DAD: Ouch! I thought you would come up with something easy, like doing your Physics homework. Oh well, I guess there's no choice. I'll just have to take my punishment like a man.

MIKE: This is such a power trip, seeing you have to face the music like this. I hope you do something else irresponsible soon, I'm already getting ideas for your next punishment.

DAD: I can't believe it, I think I've created a monster. Don't you have homework to do?

MIKE: I do, but my room's too messy for me to be able to concentrate. Please look after it for me, will you?

DAD: All right, already ... enough rubbing it in! Let's go to your room.

REVELATION
Revelation 5:11-14

(DAD is sitting and reading, son or daughter DYLAN comes in.)

DAD: Hey there, Dylan—how was school today?

DYLAN: Boring and pointless as usual, until the strangest thing happened. And I can't seem to stop thinking about it.

DAD: Well, are you going to keep me in suspense forever? What happened? Did you get your homework done on time and give your teacher a heart attack?

DYLAN: Very funny. For your information, my homework is always done on time. Well, almost always, as long as more important things don't get in the way. Do you want to know what happened or not?

DAD: I'm sorry, I'll shut up now. Tell me, go ahead.

DYLAN: Well, we were in the hallway before the last class of the day. We were just hanging out, since it was still a few minutes before class. This kid that I've never talked to before suddenly asks me to help them get his locker open. So I walk over to see what I can do and suddenly this big heavy crate falls out of the rafters and lands right where I was standing a few seconds earlier. Nobody seemed to know how the crate got up there in the first place, but that thing could have done some serious damage to my skull. Instead of standing here and talking to you, I could be in a hospital somewhere—or worse.

DAD: Unbelievable! Of course, I'm going to have a talk with your principal and make sure there's no chance of any more near misses like this happening in your school. But like you say, you're very fortunate that you weren't hurt. So how does that make you feel?

DYLAN: Kind of weird, but good. And thankful that I'm not in serious pain right now. I also have this feeling that I need to do something.

DAD: You know what I think it is? God has plans for you and those plans do not include getting hurt by that crate. But maybe he used this near miss to get your attention.

DYLAN: He got my attention all right. But how do you think He wants to use me?

DAD: Unfortunately I can't answer that. As your dad I do have some amazing powers, but answering such a deep question isn't one of them.

DYLAN: Something just occurred to me. At church they're looking for someone to teach the Kindergarten Sunday School class. I've always liked hanging out with little kids, I think I'd like to try teaching that class.

DAD: I say go for it. You know, this may be part of God revealing what He has planned for you. This is exciting!

DYLAN: Yeah, it kind of is. One thing's for sure, it's a lot better than lying in a hospital bed with a fractured skull or something. Well, if I'm going to try teaching Sunday School, I'd better make sure I get my homework done.

(DYLAN exits.)

DAD: *(Looks up.)* Lord, You reveal Yourself in the most amazing ways. Protecting Dylan from harm, creating this interest in Sunday School work and then doing homework without any threats or blackmail from me. Thank you.

Youth

REVEALING GOD'S LOVE
Psalms 36:7-10

(Two teenaged girls are discussing upcoming plans.)

JOAN: Hey Jane, what's up? You should come and hang out with our youth group tonight, it's really going to be fun!

JANE: Are you talking to me? I can't believe you're talking to me! Are you forgetting that I'm the one that spread all those nasty rumours about how you got real friendly with that guy Danny?

JOAN: I know exactly what you did and it did bother me for a bit. But I figure, hey, life is short. You messed up, but you're still one of my best friends. That's not going to change.

JANE: Wow. I can't believe you're being this nice to me! Everyone else who found out what I did is ignoring me like I have some contagious disease, except you—and you're the one I hurt the most. I promise I'll never shoot my mouth off like that again. All I was doing was trying to impress some popular kids with some juicy gossip. I am so sorry. I've learned my lesson big-time.

JOAN: That's good to hear. Because if you ever did pull something like that again, I would be forced to seriously hurt you. *(Pause.)* Just kidding!

JANE: Message received loud and clear. But I keep thinking, if you did something like this to me, I would freeze you right out of my life forever. Why haven't you done something drastic like that to me?

JOAN: Well, I think it's mostly because of my relationship with Jesus Christ. It isn't just about going to church on Sunday mornings. It's like He's becoming more and more a part of my life, and making me realize that if I ignore you now, all it would do is make both of us miserable. I just don't want to do that.

JANE: That's pretty deep. If that's the kind of thing that's going on at your youth group, I think I *will* join you tonight, if the offer is still good. Besides, I heard you guys have a fun bunch of kids.

JOAN: Awesome! I'm so glad you're coming. You're right, we are a fun group, and you never know, you might learn something real important. Let's go!

(They leave together.)

(JODY approaches Sunday School TEACHER after class.)

JODY: Excuse me, could I talk to you for a minute?

TEACHER: Sure, your name was Jody, right?

JODY: That's right. Even though it was my first time in this class, it wasn't all that boring.

TEACHER: Thanks for the compliment, I think. You said you wanted to talk to me, so what's up?

JODY: Well, I haven't spent much time at this church or any other church, either. But just now I was paging through the Bible you gave me for the class and I noticed one place where it said something like, "I will make you fishermen." From what I know about Jesus, He seems pretty cool and I would like to do what He says. But if He wants me to go fishing, will there be cell phone service where we're going? I want to make sure my friends can get hold of me if something important comes up.

TEACHER: *(Smiles.)* Actually, the verse is "I will make you fishers of men." Jesus isn't referring to actually going fishing with a rod and reel.

JODY: I see, so it's like symbolism. You know, there's this boy at school who's pretty hot, I wouldn't mind reeling him in. I could be a fisher of men and get him to ask me out.

TEACHER: If there's a boy you like and you want to get to know him better, great. But that's not exactly what Jesus is referring to here. He's encouraging us to live according to His will and provide a good example so that others will accept His message. Often that will lead to them asking Jesus to forgive their sins and accepting Him as their personal Lord and Saviour. For example, why are you here today?

JODY: My friend Terry asked me. She said it's a pretty fun class and you learn how to be a better person at the same time.

TEACHER: There you go. Terry was following what Jesus said, that we should be fishers of men—and women, in this case.

JODY: So what Jesus is telling me is to see if I can bring some of my friends to Sunday School so I can be a fisher of men and women?

TEACHER: That's one way of doing it. But you can also learn more about Jesus yourself and use that to become one of His followers; be nice to people and spread His love to everyone you meet. That's another way to be a fisher of men and women.

JODY: Thanks for explaining that to me. I would love to learn more about Jesus. And I think it'll be a lot more fun than sitting on a cold boat in the middle of a boring lake with no cell phone service. See you next Sunday. *(JODY exits.)*

AWAITING OUR SAVIOUR
Mark 11:1-11

(JESSIE sits alone, looking depressed. JESUS walks in.)

JESUS: Hey.

JESSIE: Hey.

JESUS: Mind if I sit down?

JESSIE: It's a free country, do whatever you want. Who are you anyway?

JESUS: Just someone who wants to be your friend.

JESSIE: That's not an answer, I asked who you are.

JESUS: I am Jesus, son of God.

JESSIE: Yeah, right. And I'm the Pope.

JESUS: I hate it when people don't believe I am Who I say I am. All right, I guess I'll have to embarrass you and prove who I am. Let's see, about an hour ago your girlfriend dumped you. You had been going together for two weeks, but she said she's not ready for a serious relationship and wants to see other people and now you feel like you've been kicked in the stomach. Do you believe in Me now?

JESSIE: Wow! Sure I believe you, there's no other way you could know all that stuff. *(Pause.)* But that doesn't change the fact that my life is over. I was having such a good time with her, how could she do this to me?

JESUS: Well, let's see if we can figure out why this happened.

JESSIE: Wait a minute, why are You trying to help me?

JESUS: Because I know what it's like to suffer—and I want to take away your pain. So, what do you know about her?

JESSIE: That's easy. I know that she's hot.

JESUS: What else?

JESSIE: What else *is* there?

JESUS: Hel-*lo*! I'm talking about things that you find out by talking to her and listening to her. Like what's her favourite colour? What does she like to do for fun? What are her dreams for the future? Stuff like that.

JESSIE: So you mean I should've gotten to know her, like a real person?

JESUS: Exactly! And really try to make her happy, instead of just thinking about yourself all the time. It's too bad you messed up that relationship, but do you think you can try these ideas the next time you meet someone you like?

JESSIE: I don't see why not. So you think girls really go for that kind of stuff?

JESUS: Trust me, they do. It'll make you a lot happier too if you bring joy to someone else. But remember, people are only human, no matter how good they look. Everybody makes mistakes. But if you want someone you can trust to always be there for you, just count on Me. You won't be able to always see Me, but I'll be there with you when you're reading the Bible or praying or just helping people who are having a rough time.

JESSIE: That's a deal. Would it be OK if I passed some of your good advice on to my friends?

JESUS: That would be very cool. Go for it!

JESSIE: I'd better get started. See you around.

(JESUS watches as JESSIE leaves, JESUS leaves in opposite direction.)

GOD PROVIDES
Luke 13:31-35

(Youth LEADER is on stage, teenaged CHRIS walks past, Youth LEADER stops him.)

LEADER: Hey Chris, can I talk to you for a bit?

CHRIS: Sure, if it doesn't take too long. We're getting ready for a possibly historic moment for our youth group. We're trying to see if we can beat the record for jamming people into the church storage room, which is 24. And since I'm the newest member, everyone decided that I should be record-breaking number 25. So I'm pretty pumped.

LEADER: I definitely don't want to delay history in the making, so I'll keep this short. It sounds like you're having a good time with the group.

CHRIS: Oh yeah, it's the absolute best. I really want to thank you for letting me know about your group.

LEADER: You're quite welcome. I'm just happy you actually showed up when we invited you. So you don't regret your decision to join our group?

CHRIS: Not at all. It might be the smartest thing I've ever done. Before I met you guys I would just sit at home and be bitter when all the kids from school were out having fun except me because our family couldn't afford it. And sometimes I didn't feel safe, because our neighbourhood was pretty dangerous. It was getting to the point where I just didn't feel like getting up in the morning, I felt so alone. But that's all changed. It started when your youth group worked at the soup kitchen one night when our family came in for something to eat. You invited us to your church and it was so cool because you didn't care that we didn't have any money.

LEADER: I remember that day well. Afterwards the kids made it a youth group project to pray for you and your family.

CHRIS: Those prayers have definitely paid off. I have a whole bunch of new friends. And I don't feel alone any more because I know no matter what, Jesus loves me.

LEADER: Wait a minute, you just mentioned your "old neighbourhood." Does that mean you've found a new place to live?

CHRIS: You bet, another answer to prayer. Our family can finally afford a new place in an area where it's actually safe to be outside.

LEADER: Well, praise the Lord! You know, our youth group is richer too, just for having you in it.

CHRIS: Thanks, but I've got to get back to the
                  room jam and see how they're doing.

LEADER: I think I'll come along and do an official
                  head count. Because after all, we set the
                  record you're trying to break when I was
                  close to your age.

CHRIS: *(Looks at youth leader.)* Somehow that
                  doesn't surprise me. I'll bet the whole
                  thing was your idea, wasn't it.

LEADER: *(Hesitates.)* I guess it can't hurt to admit it
                  now. Yeah, it was me. But records are
                  made to be broken, so let's go.

(They exit.)

(MR. DAWSON and teenaged KELLY walk in from opposite sides, meet Centre Stage.)

DAWSON: Hey, Kelly, how're you doing? I haven't seen you around much lately. What are you busy with these days?

KELLY: Well, Mr. Dawson, tonight I'm volunteering at the personal care home. No wait, that might be tomorrow night. Tonight the youth group is having Bible Study at church. I'm pretty sure that's tonight, or maybe tonight I'm singing in the choir concert at school. I'm sorry, I don't have my daytimer with me so I'm not real sure exactly what's going on.

DAWSON: Are you always this busy?

KELLY: Actually, this is probably my slowest time of the year. In a month or so, things are going to get a little crazy.

DAWSON: Well, it seems pretty crazy to me already. How do you do it, having so many things on the go at once?

KELLY: I try to just concentrate on one thing at a time and block everything else out. If I look too far ahead, my head will probably explode.

DAWSON: We definitely don't want *that* to happen.

KELLY: No kidding. Usually it's fun being busy, but there is one thing that's been bugging me lately.

DAWSON: What's the problem? Maybe I can help.

KELLY: I'm not even exactly sure how to say this, I just haven't felt God's presence in my life the last while and I really miss that.

DAWSON: That's hardly surprising, since you've been worried about your head exploding and all.

KELLY: Stop making fun of me.

DAWSON: I'm sorry, but you're so busy I'm getting a headache just thinking about it. I'm pretty sure God approves of the things you're involved with, but there is something missing. If you really want to feel God's presence more, I think it's still possible.

KELLY: If you're suggesting I start going to some kind of an extra class or something, I don't think I could handle that.

DAWSON: I don't think so either, and besides, then we'd be back to that same problem with your exploding head. But I think all you need to do is set aside maybe 5 or 10 minutes a day and spend that time doing nothing but reading the Bible and praying. Tell God what's going on in your life, the good stuff and the bad. Ask Him for His help with the bad stuff and thank Him for the good stuff. That opens the door for Him to really become a bigger part of your life.

KELLY: 5 or 10 minutes? I think I could handle that. Let's see, I could do it after school before choir practice starts. Or maybe between supper and homework, or possibly after I study for teaching the Kindergarten Sunday School class. But I could also maybe find time when—

(MR. DAWSON interrupts.)

DAWSON: I'm sure you'll figure it out, and it'll be worth it in the long run.

KELLY: Thanks for your help. But I need to go find my daytimer. Without that thing, I think my head really would explode.
(KELLY exits.)

(MR. DAWSON watches KELLY LEAVE, smiles, shakes his head, exits the opposite way.)

PEER PRESSURE
Romans 12:2

(Two teenaged girls enter, start talking.)

MAXINE: So is everything ready for your big party this weekend?

SANDY: Oh yeah—and everyone is going to be there, all of the cool people. The only place you could possibly find more cool people would be in a Hollywood movie.

MAXINE: Uh oh, here comes one of the *un*-cool.

(DENISE enters, approaches them.)

DENISE: Hey, guys! Sandy, I hear there's going to be a party at your place this weekend—do you think I could come?

SANDY: I seriously doubt it, you have to be cool to be invited to this party.

MAXINE: Now just hang on a second. She *might* be cool, I just don't know. Tell you what, Denise, you prove your coolness to us and you're invited—and I know just how you can do it. You know that girl in our class who gets the highest marks in everything?

DENISE: Yeah, her name's Cindy. I can't believe how smart she is.

MAXINE: Well let's see how smart she *really* is. We have a history test in a couple of days. You swipe her history text book and notes, bring it to me by the end of today and you're invited to the party.

DENISE: But without her book and notes, she won't be able to study.

MAXINE: That's right, and then maybe she won't think she's better than the rest of us.

DENISE: You know, doing this won't make me cool, just really mean. If this is what it takes to come to your party, I'm not interested.

SANDY: Let me get this straight—you're blowing off possibly the party of the year just because you have to do something a little nasty?

DENISE: Yeah, I guess I am.

SANDY: Well, that's *your* loss. Max, let's scram before this gets any more dramatic.

MAXINE: You go, I'll catch up with you in a bit.

SANDY: OK, but don't forget about that kid who was giving us a hard time yesterday. After school we're going to stuff that little pest into a locker. It's going to be hilarious.

MAXINE: I haven't forgotten. I'll see you later.

(MAXINE watches SANDY leave, turns back to DENISE when she's gone.)

DENISE: So what happens now, you gonna beat me up?

MAXINE: No, actually I wanted to tell you I admire you for what you just did.

DENISE: What? Am I hearing you right?

MAXINE: You sure are. You see, a while back some so-called cool people gave me the same kind of mean dare I just gave you, but I caved in and did it just so I could hang out with them. How come you stood up to us and said no?

DENISE: Well, I think a lot of it comes from the church I go to and our youth group there. We learn a lot about Jesus, and the thing that always stays with me is how we should try and be nice to people. I just find that if people around me are happy, life is a lot more fun. Our youth group does a lot of fun stuff together too, like movie nights and playing games or just hanging out. You should come sometime.

MAXINE: You know what, I think I will. I've got to admit, you *are* very cool. A few minutes ago I was putting pressure on you and now you're inviting me to hang out with you. I'd really like to find out more about what makes you so tough.

DENISE: You may call it toughness, I just call it God's faithfulness. For a second there I thought you were going to punch me in the teeth and now we're talking about going to youth group. It seems like God's always there, looking out for me. But for now we'd better get back to school. I don't know about you, but I need to find some extra time to study for that history test.

MAXINE: You and me both. Let's go.

(They exit.)

BRINGING PEACE IN DIFFICULT TIMES
Romans 12:17-21

(DAN is pacing back and forth at school. DOUG walks in.)

DOUG: Hey Dan, how's it going?

DAN: Lousy. Just don't talk to me if you know what's good for you.

DOUG: Whoa, what's got into you? You look like you're about ready to break somebody's neck!

DAN: Good. I'd hate to be this ticked off and not show it.

DOUG: So what's the problem or maybe I should change that to *who's* the problem?

DAN: It's that stupid idiot, Rick. Remember how I water-bombed those snobby kids from my class the other day? Well, he told the principal and now I've got two weeks' detention. I'm gonna kill him. I'll hit him so hard, he'll think it's next week!

DOUG: Hang on just a second there, tough guy. First, the water bombing was a thing of beauty. I saw it and I haven't laughed so hard in a long time. But have you thought through what will happen to you if you beat up this guy, Rick?

DAN: No, I haven't. Actually right now I'm too mad to think.

DOUG: Well, right now everyone thinks that whole water bombing thing was cool. If you beat up this guy, a lot of them will feel sorry for him and think you're a jerk. And he'll probably go straight to the principal and get you more detention, or worse.

DAN: Okay, you're probably right. But if I'm not gonna beat him up, I've at least gotta get him back somehow. You got any ideas?

DOUG: Well, you can't water bomb him because that'll only get you into more trouble. How about this? I know his locker is close to yours. Have a water balloon in your locker. Sometime when he's looking at you, take out the water balloon, and look at him like he's next on your list. It'll make him so jumpy he won't even think about being a tattletale for a while. Of course, you'll have to get rid of the water balloon right after that because he'll probably tell on you and get the principal or someone else to search your locker for evidence. What do you think?

DAN: I like that. I think that'll make me feel a lot better, hopefully without any more detention. Thanks a lot, man, for keeping me from getting into more trouble. I really appreciate it.

DOUG: Happy to help. (Pause.) I just thought of something. Our youth group at church is getting together this Saturday night to hang out, play games, stuff like that. You want to come?

DAN: Well, normally I would say no, but this church stuff seems to have made you kind of a fun guy. I could use some more of that myself.

DOUG: Cool. But we'd better get to school. If we're late they might think we're off planning pranks or something!

(They exit.)

RECOGNIZING OPPORTUNITIES
Ephesians 2:11-18

(MR. WATSON walks in, sees teenaged CHRIS sitting alone looking depressed.)

WATSON: Excuse me, is everything OK?

CHRIS: (Looks up.) What, why do you care?

WATSON: I just noticed that you don't look real happy and I want to help if I can.

CHRIS: Why, who are you, my mother?

WATSON: Good one, but I'll bet that didn't make you feel any better, did it?

CHRIS: No, my life is over. What am I going to do?

WATSON: Oh, I'm sure it's not that bad. What happened, did you find a new pimple on your face?

CHRIS: If you're trying to be funny, it's not working.

WATSON: OK, I'll make you a deal. I'll quit trying to be funny if you tell me what's wrong. Since I've never met you before, it might be easier to tell me than someone you know. And besides, it'll make you feel better to talk about it.

CHRIS: Oh all right. Things can't get any worse. Last weekend I was out with some friends and we all had a bit too much to drink. I don't remember much after that, but someone got hold of a gun somehow, and I don't know who came up with the idea to rob a convenience store, but that's what we did. And then the cops caught us about 10 minutes later. Like I said, my life is over.

WATSON: Wow. That's a tough situation. Do you know yet what your punishment is going to be?

CHRIS: No. I wish the cops or the judge or whoever would get it over with already and tell me what's going on. The not knowing is almost worse than any punishment. And my parents, they've hardly said a word to me since it happened. Usually when I mess up, they're quick to think up some kind of a punishment. But this time, it's like they're ready to give up on me.

WATSON: So why are you sitting here all alone?

CHRIS: My parents are working. Everyone who was with me that night, I think their parents have locked them up or something. All my other so-called friends, they don't want to be seen with me. It's like I'm contagious or something.

WATSON: It seems to me your biggest problem right now is too much time to think. I may have a way to help you with that. You interested?

CHRIS: Sure, spending all this time alone with nothing to do but think is driving me nuts.

WATSON: OK, here's the deal. I teach Sunday School and the kids in my class are about your age. They're always hearing from adults about how drinking can mess you up, but I'm worried they're not getting the message. If they heard it from you, someone their own age, it might get through to them.

CHRIS: You've got to be kidding! Me, get up in front of people and talk? I would have no idea what to say.

WATSON: Simple. You tell them what you just told me. How it all started with a few drinks and ended up with you robbing a store and getting caught. Just think, you might help some of them avoid the same kind of trouble you're in.

CHRIS: You know, that would be pretty cool. What happened to me has been so horrible and it would really mean a lot to me if I could save even one person from that kind of grief. OK, when do you want me to do it?

WATSON: Right now. I'm on my way there. The church is just a short walk from here.

CHRIS: I'm ready as I'll ever be. I actually have a chance to help someone. It's amazing, but I'm starting to feel a bit better. Thanks for sticking your nose into my business.

WATSON: Happy to help. But you're helping me too. I'm pretty sure today's Sunday School lesson will have a much bigger impact on the kids than if I spent the whole class talking. Let's go.

(They exit.)

(TEACHER sits at his desk, SABRINA approaches him.)

SABRINA: Excuse me, could I talk to you for a minute?

TEACHER: Sure, anytime. By the way, I really appreciate that you've been coming to our Sunday School class lately. You have a great way of livening up the discussion.

SABRINA: Thanks, that really means a lot to me. But what I want to talk to you about is—well, I need to ask you something. I became a Christian about a month ago and at first it was just wonderful. It felt like Jesus was constantly so close, like He was right next to me. I thought He would just keep getting closer and closer to me, but lately it's been kind of the opposite. I don't feel His nearness as much, and I miss it. What do I do?

TEACHER: Well, I like to compare our Christian faith to a two-way street. Of course Jesus wants to get closer and closer to us, but at the same time, we have to really make an effort to get closer to Him. So how have you been trying to get closer to Jesus?

SABRINA: Well, I've been coming to Sunday School, doesn't that mean I'm making the effort?

TEACHER: It's a start. But that's like one hour out of each week. To really get closer to Jesus, you need to spend more time at it than that. Let's start with music. How much music do you listen to in an average day?

SABRINA: Lets's see, I wish we could have tunes going during school, but for some strange reason the teachers don't let us do that. But after school, in the evening, I have the music going pretty well all the time—I'd say three or four hours every day.

TEACHER: OK, let's be conservative and call it three hours per day of music. Out of all of that, how much music do you listen to that has a Christian message?

SABRINA: Well, to be honest, in a typical day I rarely listen to *any* Christian music.

TEACHER: Sounds like someone else I know. When I was your age it was basically the same thing; I had the tunes going all the time and it was rarely Christian music. I was a bit of a metal head. But eventually that music would play over and over in my head even when the stereo wasn't on, and I realized that I didn't want that stuff in my head all the time. So I started listening to more Christian music and less of the other stuff and all of a sudden my mind was freed up to think about things that really matter.

SABRINA: Are you telling me to totally give up listening to the radio, stuff like that?

TEACHER: That's completely up to you. What I'm suggesting is a better balance. If you start listening to even just a few minutes of Christian music each day and less of the other stuff, you'll have no choice but to feel closer to Jesus. And I'm sure that pretty soon you'll want to listen to even more Christian music, to read the Bible more, pray more—all those good things where Jesus can speak to you and bring you closer to Him.

SABRINA: I can't believe I never thought of it that way. That really makes a lot of sense.

TEACHER: And as you do all those things, that closeness you feel to Jesus will become obvious to people around you, and I believe you'll soon be spreading His love to everyone you meet.

SABRINA: The way you describe it, it seems so natural. I can't wait to give it a try. Thanks a lot for listening to me.

TEACHER: Thank *you* for asking. I'm sure the Lord is going to do great things in your life. See you next Sunday School class.

(They exit.)

EXCUSES, EXCUSES
1 Peter 2:9-10

(RON is sitting alone in his living room, quite pleased with himself.)

RON: I am so brilliant! Everyone at church was trying to rope me into helping out with the fundraiser tonight for the new refugees from Iraq, but I was too smart for them. What a great idea, telling them I promised my friend to help fix his truck because he needs it for work tomorrow and he can't wait on his mechanic. I mean, who's going to check up on me when they're all at church? Now I get to watch the game just like I planned, with no distractions.

TORI: *(knocks on the door and looks in.)* Hi, can I come in?

RON: Oh sure, come on in, Terry.

TORI: Actually my name's Tori, but you're close. I have a favour to ask you. I'm working on some chemistry homework that I just don't get and it's due for tomorrow. No one else is home at our house and since everyone knows you're the smartest person on our street, I thought I'd check with you. Do you think you could help me with it?

RON: *(Pauses, nervously looks at his watch.)* Well, normally I'd love to, Terry—I mean Tori—but I have been fighting a major migraine headache for the last couple of days. The doctor gave me some pills and told me to relax and not "strain my brain" in any way and, as you know, chemistry involves a lot of that. Sorry I can't help.

TORI: *(Looks disappointed.)* Oh, don't worry about it. I guess I'll have to figure it out by myself. *(Starts walking out the door.)* I hope you feel better soon. Bye.

RON: Good luck with that chemistry. *(Makes sure she's gone.)* Boy, that was close. It's a good thing I'm so quick on my feet. migraine headache, I'll have to remember that for future use. *(Checks watch.)* Good thing that didn't take too long, the game should be just getting started.

DANNY: *(Knocks on the door and looks in.)* Hi, can I come in?

RON: Oh sure, come on in, Donny. *(Again looks nervously at watch.)*

DANNY: Actually my name's Danny, but you're close. I need to ask you something. Our soccer team has a big game tomorrow morning and I'm the goalie. I could really use some practise, but no one else is around. I was wondering if you could take some shots on me.

RON: You mean right now?

DANNY: That would probably be best since it'll be getting dark soon. Could you do it for me, just this once?

RON: I would really like to help you out, Donny—I mean Danny—but I don't think this old body of mine is up to it. I hurt my knees back when I played football and anytime I start kicking soccer balls around they really bother me so bad sometimes I can barely walk. I'm really sorry.

DANNY: *(Looks disappointed.)* Oh, that's okay. I'll have to see if I can find someone else. See you later. *(DANNY leaves.)*

RON: Why does everyone in this neighbourhood think I can solve all their problems? Oh well, let's turn on the game. *(Clicks remote, lights go off.)* What *is* this? Why does the power have to go off *now* when I'm trying to watch the game? Maybe it won't take long, sometimes it comes back on in a few seconds. It's not coming back on.

I know what this is. Lord, you're trying to get my attention here, aren't You. Okay, I'll admit, lately I *have* been focusing on myself and what *I* want, and not taking advantage of opportunities to spread Your love to those around me. Tell You what, from now on, watching sports can wait if there's someone who really needs my help. No more lame excuses.

You know, Lord, it's kind of neat to know that You have chosen me to help others. *(Heads for the door and calls offstage.)* Danny, you still out there? My knees are actually feeling pretty good tonight. Where's that soccer ball, let's see how good of a goalie you are.

(RON exits.)

GOD SEES OUR NEED
Revelation 7:9-17

(Teenaged MAX is sitting, deep in thought. Youth Leader MR. HARRIS approaches.)

MR. HARRIS: Hey Max, I'm glad you could make it tonight to party it up with the rest of the youth. But why are you sitting here all by yourself? Is there something wrong?

MAX: Oh no, in fact it's exactly the opposite. I feel great, I'm having a good time just sitting here watching people have fun.

MR. HARRIS: I'm glad to hear that. So are you going to tell me what's got you in such a good mood or do I have to guess?

MAX: It would take you about 100 years to guess and I don't have that much time so I'll tell you. The way it started off, I thought it would be a total disaster. I thought my best friend Terry, who I've known forever, was going to have to move away. Terry's dad lost his job due to "downsizing," or whatever the word is these days when someone works for a heartless company for about 20 years and they just kick him out the door for no good reason. Anyway, Terry's dad was having no luck finding another job so they were getting ready to move away someplace where his chances might be better. Terry just hated the idea, and I wasn't exactly thrilled about it, either.

MR. HARRIS: I can see where that would be very tough to take. You two are together so much, sometimes I think I might have to use a crowbar to pry you apart. Too bad Terry couldn't make it tonight. So anyway, you said their family almost had to move away. What happened?

MAX: It was the most amazing thing. They had an interested buyer for their house and were ready to close the deal when Terry's dad got this incredible phone call. Another local company told him they had a position open up that same day doing the same type of work Terry's dad had always done—and at almost exactly the same pay. It seems impossible, but it actually happened!

MR. HARRIS: Unbelievable! The Lord sure works in some mysterious and wonderful ways.

MAX: You got that right! But it makes me wonder, I mean God is so amazing and powerful and awesome and Terry and I are just regular people. Why would He do something this incredible for us?

MR. HARRIS: That's the thing about God. He's all-knowing and all-powerful, and sometimes the way He works is just too much for our puny little human brains to comprehend. However, I do have my own theory on a possible reason He did this for you guys.

MAX: I can't wait to hear this.

MR. HARRIS: Well, let's look at the facts. It looked like you and Terry would be separated, but at the last minute God kept that from happening. So I just have this feeling that somewhere down the road, you two are going to accomplish something so amazing and pleasing to God, something that would have been impossible if you had been split up.

MAX: Cool! You know Mr. Harris, in the past I've thought that some of your theories and ideas were a little bit strange and warped, but I do like this one. I wonder what God has planned for us.

MR. HARRIS: I must admit, I'm curious myself. But he'll reveal all that to you when the time is right. In the meantime, I see the rest of the group is getting ready to play "Sardines." *(Looks offstage then back to MAX.)* Are you ready to join them?

MAX: Let's do it. *(Yells offstage.)* Hey you guys, I'm hiding first!

(MAX runs offstage, MR. HARRIS moves to follow.)

MR. HARRIS: All right everyone, let's not turn into raving lunatics here. Tell you what, I'm thinking of a number between one and 47.6. Whoever guesses the closest to it, gets to hide first.

(He exits.)

Work

Genesis 39:1-22

(Setting: The office after a tough week at work. JAMES enters.)

JAMES: Boy, am I glad that this week is over. This job of mine is sure wearing me out these days. I am so glad the weekend is here! I think I'll just head down to the bar with the office crowd and have a few tall cool ones to help me unwind. After a few drinks maybe I'll have a few more and just kind of forget about how difficult work is, how stressful it is at home with two teenaged kids, and all the rest of it. But then, that's basically what I do just about every Friday night.

I keep thinking about this guy at work, I think his name's Paul. His life must be incredibly dull. He goes to church at least once a week and never comes out to the bar no matter how often we ask him.

I don't know what he does for fun—or if he even knows what fun means. But on the other hand, he must enjoy his life because he seems to have a smile on his face all the time. He's always nice to everyone around here, including that girl Elaine, who is just as annoying as listening to fingernails on a blackboard. Most of us have a hard time just talking to her with a straight face. And Paul works harder than almost anyone around here, yet he never complains. What's his secret?

cont'd ...

Maybe I should ask him sometime. Naw, I couldn't do that, what if someone sees me? Everyone would just make jokes and laugh at me. But on the other hand, what do I care? Waking up with a hangover every Saturday morning is not exactly the highlight of my life. If I could somehow lighten up and even smile more often like Paul does, I'll bet work would be less stressful and life in general would be a lot easier. Where is that guy? Just thinking about talking to him is already making me feel better.

(JAMES exits.)

Luke 4:1-13

(Co-workers DAVE and RICK walk in, RICK starts talking.)

RICK: So Dave, what did you do over the weekend?

DAVE: Oh, not much, just watched a bunch of sports. It was nice to be lazy for a change.

RICK: I know what you mean. I can't believe it's Monday already.

DAVE: I think Mondays should be outlawed. It is so hard to get motivated to come back to work.

RICK: Normally I would agree with you 100 per cent. But today is a more interesting Monday than usual. Did you see Jeff down in shipping this morning?

DAVE: Sure, but what's so interesting about that?

RICK: Did you notice the shirt he was wearing? I mean Jeff is not exactly a slim guy anymore and that shirt is so tight, you can see pretty much every one of those pounds he's put on. It's really funny. We need to come up with a nice, descriptive nickname for him. Let's see—Gorilla Gut or the Round Mound of Downtown, or maybe something else, what do you think?

DAVE: I know it's tempting to laugh at someone like that and make fun of them, but I don't think it's a good idea. How would you like it if I told everyone about how you offered to wash the boss' car, just so he would let you help him put together a big presentation. I bet someone would come up with a real colourful nickname for you, like maybe "Vacuum Cleaner" because you seem to be sucking up all the time.

RICK: You wouldn't dare! You promised me you'd never tell anyone about that.

DAVE: I know, and I plan to keep that promise—most likely anyway. But now you have an idea how Jeff feels. That's why I don't think we or anyone else should cut people down, including Jeff. Maybe he can't afford to buy a whole new wardrobe since he put on some weight. It's really none of our business.

RICK: All right, all right. You sure have changed. A while back you would have been the first to jump all over Jeff and make all kinds of fat jokes. What happened?

DAVE: Jesus happened. Studying His Word has taught me a lot of things, including how important it is to treat people right. It's tempting to make jokes and criticize, but that's no way to live. I prefer to build people up instead of tear them down.

RICK: Wow. You have definitely given me something to think about.

DAVE: Well, I've got to get back to work. I'll see you at lunch.

(DAVE exits.)

RICK: Who does he think he is, getting all over me just for making a joke. *(Pauses to think.)* I've got to admit though, Dave seems a lot happier than he used to be. I wonder if he was just messing with me or if Jesus really is the reason why. I'll have to ask him at lunch.

(RICK exits.)

FAITH AT WORK
Luke 13:1-9

(TOM is deep in thought, doesn't see co-worker TIM approach.)

TIM: Hi, Tom, you ready for another busy day at work?

TOM: Oh, hey Tim. Yeah sure. *(Pauses.)* Wait a minute, you're talking to me, how is that possible? After what I did to you, I thought you might pull out a gun and shoot me or something.

TIM: Oh, come on, it wasn't that bad. Everyone makes mistakes.

TOM: This wasn't just a mistake. You showed me your great idea for the ad campaign for our new client and I stole it and tried to take the credit. I was trying to take money out of your pocket. That's about as bad as it gets.

TIM: What's done is done. Forget it, as long as you've learned your lesson.

TOM: Oh, you can count on that. For a few extra dollars, it's just not worth it. I felt so bad, it was almost a relief when you found out. I never, ever want to go through that again.

TIM: That's settled, then. And besides, it sounds like you learned something. I think the old saying is really true: our best lessons come from our own mistakes.

TOM: There's one thing I don't get. How can you be so nice to me when I tried to steal your idea and make money that was rightfully yours?

TIM: That comes from my faith in Jesus Christ. He taught that I should love my neighbour and do unto others as I would have them do unto me. Then He died on the cross for all our sins—so compared to that, it's not that big of a deal for me to forgive you.

TOM: That is really deep. It sure gives me lots to think about and I would really like to talk to you some more about this sometime. But right now, I need to get to work.

TIM: Me too. Speaking of work, I was wondering if you could take a look at another ad campaign I'm working on. I think I've got a good basic concept, but I'm having trouble fleshing it out. If you want to take a shot at it, meet me at my office in about half an hour. *(TIM leaves.)*

TOM: *(As TIM leaves)* Oh, I'll definitely be there. *(After TIM is gone.)* Unbelievable! After I basically stabbed him in the back, he still wants to work with me. This Jesus Christ he talks about must be one powerful dude!

(TOM exits.)

(MR. GARNER is sitting at his office desk, hears a knock on his door from new employee FREDDY. MR. GARNER is not pleased.)

FREDDY: *(Knocks on door and looks in.)* Excuse me, I'm looking for the lunchroom.

GARNER: Does this look like a lunchroom? What's the matter with you? How did you get in here anyway? Why didn't my secretary stop you?

FREDDY: I just saw her leave, something about picking up her boss's drycleaning. And I'll bet you're the boss, right?

GARNER: *(Sarcastic.)* Good call, Sherlock. And who in the world are you? Never mind that, I think I'll go find a security guard and have you thrown out.

(MR. GARNER stands up, sits back down when FREDDY starts talking.)

cont'd ...

FREDDY: Please don't do that. My name is Freddy Carson. I just started working here a couple of days ago. And I'm not really looking for the lunchroom. I wanted to tell you something about your company. You sell all kinds of electronics and gadgets that are mostly meant for high school kids. Your stuff was pretty cool a few years ago, and I even bought some of it. But lately, you're losing touch, man. You do all this advertising telling kids to buy all this stuff, but you really don't know what they want anymore. Times are changing and you need to talk *at* the kids less and start listening *to* them more. If I'm going to keep working here, I want to make sure this company is ready for the future.

GARNER: You know what? I'm glad I didn't have you thrown out. Sales have been down the last little while and while I don't know that you necessarily have all the answers, your ideas are certainly worth considering. Tell me, have you always been this bold?

FREDDY: No, I used to be really shy. I had a lot of trouble talking to people and I never said anything to strangers. I was just really scared that people wouldn't like me. But I kept seeing how people who took chances usually ended up making friends and doing well in whatever they tried. I really wanted that for myself, so I prayed to God about it and He helped me slowly overcome my shyness. Without His help, there's no way I'd be here talking to you right now.

GARNER: So you pray to God. Do you go to church, too?

FREDDY: Oh yeah. It's a great way to learn about God and learn from other people who also believe in him.

GARNER: That's very interesting. Until now, I thought it was a crutch people used when they weren't strong enough to compete in the real world. But you're not like that. You have some real potential, Freddy Carson. If you work hard, I think you could really do well working here. The next time we have an opening in our marketing department, I'm definitely going to keep you in mind.

FREDDY: I'd really appreciate that, sir. You know, after meeting you, I could see myself working here for a long time.

GARNER: That's what I like to hear. And you know what else I'm going to do? From now on, when our personnel department recommends we hire someone, I'm going to ask if they go to church. We could use some more of that confidence and boldness you've learned.

FREDDY: Cool! *(Looks at watch.)* Well, I'd better get to work, I don't want to make the boss mad.

(FREDDY exits.)

cont'd ...

GARNER: *(MR. GARNER smiles and watches him leave.)* I should really start going to church again. I don't think I've gone since back before I graduated business school. It really looks like I've been missing something special.

(PAT walks in, JERRY'S muttering to himself, shaking his head.)

PAT: Hey Jerry, how's it going today?

JERRY: Horrible! Don't even talk to me if you know what's good for you. I am possibly in the worst mood in the history of the world!

PAT: Why? What happened? You never know, it might help to talk about it.

JERRY: OK, you asked for it. There's this guy named Davis where I work. He's only been there a few months, while on the other hand I've been working my tail off there for years. But when a job in management opened up, they promoted Davis over me. I just don't get it.

PAT: Wow, that sounds rough. It surprises me, because I know you've got a lot of talent.

JERRY: You bet I do. I'm always coming up with good ideas. If they would just use half of my ideas instead of being such stubborn idiots, we'd be far more productive and I would be the one getting promoted.

PAT: Well, what about this Davis person. He must have been promoted for a reason.

JERRY: I don't know. From what I can tell, his biggest talent is kissing other people's butts.

PAT: That may be, but I doubt if that's what got him promoted. He must have something else going for him.

JERRY: I really couldn't tell you. There always seems to be a crowd of people in his office and everyone comes out of there in a good mood and ready to work.

PAT: It sounds to me like Davis has some natural leadership qualities. That's something very valuable when it comes to management. Jerry, do you think maybe you could benefit from trying to get along with people better?

JERRY: What? Actually be concerned about other people's lives? I suppose that wouldn't be so bad. Who knows, I might make some new friends.

PAT: Yeah, and when the next promotion comes along, it'll be a lot harder for your bosses to ignore you.

JERRY: You know, that's so radical it just might work. Thanks for talking to me, Pat, you've helped a lot. I can't help but wonder, why do you bother being nice to me, when I've been so grouchy lately?

PAT: Well, it all starts with my Christian faith. I've found that I'm a lot happier trying to help others than being so self-centred like I used to be.

JERRY: Wow, that sounds like quite a change. Do you think we could get together for coffee sometime and talk about this some more?

PAT: It would be my pleasure.

(They exit.)

FAITH & THE WORKPLACE
Ephesians 6:10-17

(JOHN and CHRIS are at work, talking.)

JOHN: Hey, Chris, how was your weekend?

CHRIS: Oh, pretty much the same as usual. It seems like nothing interesting ever happens in my life. How was your weekend?

JOHN: It was really good. I spent some time with friends and met some very interesting people. It was just what I needed to energize me for work today.

CHRIS: I sure could use some of that ambition. John, there's something I've been meaning to ask you. You know Danny in shipping?

JOHN: Sure, I've talked to him a few times.

CHRIS: Well, I was just wondering something. Danny can be such an obnoxious jerk sometimes, I often feel like punching his lights out. He can make it stressful just being at work. And yet, you're always nice to him, even friendly. How do you do it?

JOHN: For me, it's all part of being a born-again Christian.

CHRIS: Wait a minute. I know you go to church just about every Sunday. But what does that have to do with getting along with people like Danny?

JOHN: Through my relationship with Jesus Christ, I've learned a lot. One of those things is to love your neighbour as yourself. At first it can be kind of tough, but I eventually realized that I'm a lot happier being nice to people and trying to make them happy instead of letting little things get to me and stress me out.

CHRIS: Wow. Sounds complicated. I don't know if I could ever have the self-control to do something like that.

JOHN: That's the great part of it. If you put your trust in Jesus, he'll help you become a much better person than you ever thought possible.

CHRIS: You know, you've given me a lot to think about.

JOHN: Tell you what, why don't you come to church with me sometime? No pressure, you can just kind of take everything in. If you have any questions, I'll do my very best to find you the answers. If you want to just watch and listen and not say much, that's fine, too. And, I'll introduce you to some terrific people who aren't that different from you.

CHRIS: Well, I think I just might do that. It can't be any worse than letting people like Danny make me crazy.

JOHN: And you might find out something else, too. Contrary to popular opinion, a lot of born-again Christians are also fun-loving people. You never know, getting involved with us could actually put a smile on your face.

CHRIS: That's a nice thought, but I'll believe it when I see it.

JOHN: Fair enough, but for now we'd better get back to work.

(They exit.)

Outreach

LOVE ONE ANOTHER
Genesis 9:8-17

(STEVE and BRENDA walk in together after he gave her a ride home.)

BRENDA: Thank you so much for giving me a ride home after my stupid car broke down, what was your name again?

STEVE: My name's Steve and I was happy to do it.

BRENDA: Well, thanks again, Steve. I don't know how long I was out there after my car quit, it felt like hours. All kinds of vehicles drove by, but nobody stopped or even slowed down. Would it have killed them to at least ask if I was in some kind of trouble? I mean look at me, it's not like I would try to trick someone into stopping so I could rob them or something.

STEVE: Of course not, but sometimes people get in too much of a hurry and they don't really notice when someone like you needs help.

BRENDA: Bull cookies! I'm mad at just about the whole world right now, so don't try to make excuses for those inconsiderate pinheads. But you stopped and helped me out. Why would you stop when everyone else was just ignoring me?

cont'd ...

STEVE: It's probably because I'm such a considerate, loveable guy. *(BRENDA smiles and shakes her head.)* OK, I should have known you wouldn't buy that. Really, it's because of my Christian faith. I'm a born-again Christian, and to me that means a lot more than going to church on Sundays. It also means looking out for you and everyone else around me, like Jesus would want me to do.

BRENDA: I must admit, I didn't expect you to say that. Most people I know that go to church aren't like that. In fact, they seem kind of stuck-up, like they think they're better than me or something. But you're different.

STEVE: What's different is, Jesus is working in me. It's a gradual process, but through Him I'm becoming a much better person than I could ever hope to be all on my own. And the great thing is, Jesus can do the same thing for anybody.

BRENDA: And you say all this starts with going to church?

STEVE: That's as good a place as any to start. Tell you what, I'll tell you where our church is, and you can come on Sunday sometime for the service. I'll introduce you to some other Christians and we'll take it from there. It's really a friendly group of people.

BRENDA: Thanks for the invitation. You're really making it difficult to say no. *(She pauses and thinks.)* OK, I'll do it. You know what, you're having a good influence on me already. I was in such a bad mood only a few minutes ago, but now I'm feeling so much better.

STEVE: The Lord works in strange and wonderful ways. See you in Church!

BRENDA: Bye. And thanks again.

(STEVE exits.)

I don't know if I've ever met anyone that seems happier or more content. I wonder if Jesus could have that kind of an effect on me.

(She exits.)

HELPING THE DOWNTRODDEN
Luke 4:14-21

(JOHN walks into his house, brings DAVE—who is homeless, with him.)

DAVE: I can't believe you invited me into your house. Why would you do that, I've never met you before. I'm just a street person.

JOHN: I just felt it was the right thing to do, like the Holy Spirit was leading me. You looked like you could use a friend.

DAVE: But for all you know I could be dangerous and you still let me into this nice house.

JOHN: Well, I have faith that God knows what's best and besides, you don't look dangerous. A little grubby and wrinkled maybe, but not dangerous. *(Pause.)* I was just wondering, would you like to go to church with me this Sunday?

DAVE: There it is! I knew there was going to be a catch to this whole deal. What's next, do I have to get up in front of your whole church and let you tell them what a poor, horrible, messed-up person I am?

JOHN: Oh no, nothing like that. You see, I go to church so I can learn to follow Jesus better and then become a better person. Without His help, I never would have even had the guts to talk to you.

DAVE: In that case, Jesus is cool. So you got up the nerve to talk to me from faith in God and following the way of Jesus, right?

JOHN: I sure did. It's really amazing what's happened since I gave my life to Jesus. I used to be unhappy and mad at the world most of the time, but not anymore. I am so much happier when I do what I can to help people around me.

DAVE: This is really something. Until now, the most I heard the names of God and Jesus was when people were yelling and swearing at me. But if I came to your church, would I have to say anything?

JOHN: Not unless you want to. You would just be there to listen. If you decide to ask questions, great, but no one is going to pressure you.

DAVE: Then it's a deal, I'll go to church with you. *(Pause.)* Well, I guess I should get going.

JOHN: Wait a minute, you just got here. I don't know about you but I'm pretty hungry and I just stocked up the kitchen yesterday. How about you join me for something to eat?

DAVE: You're on, I *am* really hungry. This day just keeps getting better.

(They exit.)

THE NEW GOOD SAMARITAN
Luke 10:30-37

(JACK is sitting alone in shock after being robbed, TED approaches him.)

TED: Is everything OK?

JACK: I've just been robbed. Someone knocked me down from behind, stole my wallet and ran off. Unfortunately, he was pretty fast.

TED: Did he hurt you at all?

JACK: No, I think the only thing injured here was my pride.

TED: That's good to hear. *(Pause.)* Tell you what, let me buy you lunch and we'll figure out what to do next from there.

JACK: Thanks for stopping to help a complete stranger. You're just like the good Samaritan.

TED: Say what now?

JACK: You know, the good Samaritan, from the Bible?

TED: Oh, the Bible. I don't know much about that. It's been a long time since I've been to church.

JACK: You could've fooled me. Helping me like this is exactly the type of thing Jesus teaches in the Bible. So why don't you go to church?

TED: Oh, I used to go as a kid, but my parents said there were too many hypocrites there so they just quit taking me. I guess old habits die hard, because I've never gone back since.

JACK: Well, you're invited to our church as of right now. There's always room for good-hearted people like yourself to spread God's love and message of peace. We're far from perfect, but your good example can only help us become better people. And besides, we're having a potluck lunch after the service this Sunday. If there's one thing people in our church know how to do, it's cook. And eat, of course.

TED: Wow, I didn't expect all this from just stopping to see if you were OK. But I think I will take you up on that kind offer. I could probably learn a lot from you guys, too, including that Good Samaritan story. I'll be there Sunday. Now let's go get lunch.

(They both exit.)

WHAT WOULD JESUS DO?
John 12:20-33

(HOMELESS PERSON on stage, trying to keep warm. Well-dressed MAN walks by.)

HOMELESS PERSON: Excuse me sir, I'm very sorry to bother you, but could you help me out with some spare change?

MAN: Uh, sorry, I can't help you.

HOMELESS PERSON: Please, I haven't eaten anything since yesterday. I could really use your help.

MAN: All right, that's enough. I'm really tired of you people thinking that I am somehow obligated to support you. Here's a new approach: how about getting a job!

HOMELESS PERSON: Don't you think I've tried to find work? I haven't been able to get a job anywhere and I am so hungry.

MAN: If I help you, word will get around and then all the street people will be coming to me for money. Can't you see that's just not a workable situation? Really, I need to be going.

HOMELESS PERSON: You're all dressed up, were you in church?

MAN: Not that it's any of your business,
                        but yes, I was. It was a fine,
                        uplifting service. I was in a real
                        good mood until you came along
                        and spoiled it.

HOMELESS PERSON: So if you go to church, you must
                        believe in God. OK, I've got one
                        question and then I won't bother
                        you any more. If Jesus was here
                        today and met someone like me
                        who needed help, what would
                        Jesus do?

*(MAN walks away, HOMELESS PERSON watches and
shakes his head, then leaves.)*

OVERCOMING OBSTACLES
Acts 6:1-7

(Businessman DON is checking his watch, COREY walks in, looking uncomfortable.)

COREY: Excuse me, could you tell me what time it is?

DON: Of course. *(Looks at watch again.)* It's about 9:15.

COREY: Thanks. It's so hard to get used to, not having a watch.

DON: So what happened to yours, did you lose it?

COREY: No, actually I had to sell it. I just got out of jail a few weeks ago and, this is kind of embarrassing, but I'm short on money and it was a pretty expensive watch.

DON: Well it's obvious what you need to do: get a job.

COREY: That's what I've been trying to do, but a prison record doesn't exactly look impressive on the old resumé. I've had so many interviews where they seemed quite impressed with me, until they found out I was an ex-con. Then they all of a sudden get real stiff and give me the same old line: "Don't call us, we'll call you."

DON: That's too bad. So if you don't mind my asking, what did you do before you went to prison?

COREY: I was working for a carpenter. It was hard work, but really rewarding. I loved being able to see what I had done with my own two hands at the end of each day.

DON: So how how do you go from a fulfilling job like that to ending up in prison?

COREY: It's so stupid, I still can't believe I did it. Some friends and I were hanging out one weekend and we saw this amazing car, a 1967 Shelby Mustang GT 500, in mint condition. My buddies dared me to hotwire it, so I did. It was so much fun to drive, but that thrill lasted about 10 minutes until the cops caught me and it was all over.

DON: Wow. One little moment of bad judgement and it sure changed your life. You know, you and I aren't that different. You obviously made a mistake by stealing that car, but I've made mistakes too. The only difference is you got caught. *(DON pauses to think.)* Tell you what, I have a buddy who owns a construction company. He's been complaining about how hard it is to find good help. I'm pretty sure I could get you a job with him. What do you think? It would be hard work, but I know there's a lot of room for moving up in his company if you do a good job.

COREY: That would be awesome, it's exactly what I need! Thank you so much. Why are you doing this for me?

DON: Well, I go to church and believe what the Bible teaches and it says we're supposed to help other people who need it. And I've also got a bit of a confession to make. I've always been kind of uncomfortable about talking to ex-cons but I think that's probably because I've never talked to one until now. You're not mean or obnoxious, you're just a regular guy. So, in a way, you're also helping me.

COREY: Thanks again, you won't be sorry. If this is the kind of thing they teach in church, I think I'll stop turning down my Mom and accept her invitation the next time she invites me to go with her.

DON: Sounds great. I'll let you know after I talk to my buddy about the job. And remember, no more stealing cars.

COREY: Don't worry. I have learned my lesson big-time. Talk to you later.

(COREY leaves.)

ALL IS NOT LOST
Philippians 1:20-21

(TERRY enters, sees DAVE staring off into space.)

TERRY: Hey, Dave! I'm glad I ran into you. It's been an awfully long time since I've seen you. You looked like you were deep in thought there.

DAVE: Oh hi, Terry. Sorry, I was just thinking about my niece, Jessica. She died in a car accident a few weeks ago.

TERRY: Oh no, that's just awful. Wasn't she only about 16 years old.

DAVE: No, actually she was 19 and always full of life and saying exactly what was on her mind. Whenever she saw me it was always "Uncle Dave, you're getting old. You need a woman in your life." She was always trying to set me up with someone. It never worked out, but I loved the fact that she cared so much about me. And she was that way with everybody. I really miss her.

TERRY: Well, you and your family have my sympathy. If there's anything I can do, please let me know.

DAVE: Actually, you're helping already. Just talking about it somehow makes it easier. When it first happened there was so much going on and so many people around, there wasn't much time to think. But now, it seems like I'm always thinking about it.

TERRY: So how did it happen?

DAVE: She was just out cruising. Her friend Laura was behind the wheel, somehow lost control of the car and ran into a pole. Laura only had some minor injuries, but Jess wasn't so lucky.

TERRY: How awful for Laura.

DAVE: I know. Right after the accident, I wanted to go to the cops and have her put in jail. But after I calmed down and met her and her family, I realized that would just be wrong and no one else in our family wanted to punish her either. That poor girl is in such agony, we're just all trying to help her cope. She's a terrific and smart kid. She's apparently always wanted to be a doctor. Somehow, we've got to help her to keep going after that dream.

TERRY: Well, you are all amazing for being so understanding and supportive. There are a lot of people out there who would have nothing but vengeance on their minds in such a situation.

DAVE: Thanks, but we're not doing this alone. We've all noticed God's presence all along, He's made it so much easier. Without Him, I don't think we would have been able to let go of the anger and the hurt.

TERRY: That's great. I'll tell you right now, there're people watching how you guys are handling this. I'll bet your good example will stay with them and help them cope if they ever experience loss in their own lives. Who knows, you might even have opportunities to tell others about your faith as a result.

DAVE: I never thought of that but that would be awesome. And it would make Jess happy too, she was always full of the love of Jesus.

TERRY: Sounds like a great tribute to her memory. I'll talk to you soon. All the best to you and your family. Bye now.

(TERRY leaves.)

OVERQUALIFIED
Philippians 2:5-11

(JOHN is helping out at the soup kitchen, DOUG comes in for food, JOHN welcomes him at the door.)

JOHN: Hello, welcome here, come on in.

DOUG: Thanks, it's nice to be inside where it's warm. *(Pause, DOUG looks at JOHN intently.)* Hey, don't I know you from somewhere?

JOHN: I don't think so, I'm pretty sure we've never met before.

DOUG: No that's not it. *(Another pause.)* I know! I've seen you on TV! Sometimes, when they have cameras at the courthouse. You're a lawyer, aren't you?

JOHN: Yes, that's right. I didn't think anybody paid attention to that stuff.

DOUG: Wow, a real TV celebrity. This is pretty exciting. But if you're a lawyer and important enough to be on TV, you're making a pretty good living. So why in the world would you be working as a greeter here at the soup kitchen. I mean, I'm obviously here because I'm hungry. But aren't you kind of seriously overqualified to be here?

JOHN: I don't know about that. Jesus is the son of God and He came down to earth and died on the cross so that our sins could be forgiven and then He rose from the dead. If you think about it, the Son of God coming down to earth to live as an ordinary man, that's about as overqualified as you could be. So I'm just trying to follow His example in my own small way.

DOUG: Jesus, wow, I always thought of him as the guy in the old pictures on the wall in some church that only old people go to. So what you're saying is that Jesus has a direct influence on your life.

JOHN: He sure does. If it wasn't for Him, I likely wouldn't be here. My instincts used to tell me to just think of myself, but learning about Jesus has shown me that I'm a whole lot happier if I'm trying to help people around me.

DOUG: That sounds awesome! Do you think I could learn about Jesus, too? Just thinking about my own problems is so depressing. I would like to help others too, even though I'm not sure how much good I would be right now.

JOHN: There's always room for more, no matter what your situation is. Jesus teaches that there are a lot more important things in this world than how much money you make—or don't make. Why don't you come to our church sometime and find out more?

DOUG: I think I'll do that, it sounds like good nourishment. But right now, I'll think I'll go get some of the other kind of nourishment. Whatever they're cooking in here, it sure smells good. See you in church.

(They both exit.)

SPREADING GOD'S LIGHT
Psalm 36

(RON'S watching TV, suddenly starts throwing remote, chair and pillows.)

RON: I can't stand this! Why did Carol have to leave me? Because I acted like a total idiot, that's why! Why did I have to act like a total idiot? I am such a loser! What am I going to do?

(DON knocks on the door and looks in.)

DON: Hey Ron, is it all right if I come in?

RON: Oh sure, no problem, do whatever you want.

(DON walks in, looks around at the mess.)

DON: What happened, it looks like a hurricane just blew through here?

RON: Oh, that's nothing. Uh, you see, well it's kind of like ... the thing is—I was just watching the hockey game and once again, the Leafs managed to lose a game they should have won.

DON: Normally I would totally agree with you but there's one little problem. The Leafs didn't even play today.

RON: Oh yeah, I forgot. *(Pause.)* OK, the truth. Boy, this is not easy to talk about. My wife left me a couple days ago and I guess it's just starting to hit me that she's really gone. And with the way I treated her the last little while, I don't think she's coming back, ever.

DON: Now it's my turn for a confession. I already knew about that, so I just wanted to come by and say hello. I don't know any magic words that will suddenly make all your troubles go away, but if you ever want to hang out, do something together sometime or whatever, I'm there.

RON: Thanks, man, that might be just what I need. Hey, tomorrow night the Leafs really do have a game; I think it's against Boston. You want to come over and watch?

DON: That would be great, I'll be here. But I should warn you, I'm a Bruins fan from 'way back, so I'm not gonna go easy on you.

RON: Hey, bring it on, I wouldn't have it any other way. I'm looking forward to it.

(DON leaves.)

Wow, what a cool guy! I used to think most of the people at that church he goes to are hypocrites but maybe I was wrong about that. I wonder if what goes on at that church has anything to do with how he's trying to help me out? Maybe I should ask him, but I think I'll wait till after the Leafs embarrass those poor Bruins. *(Pause. RON smiles.)* I didn't think it was possible, but I'm actually starting to feel just a tiny bit better.

CULTURE & LIVING OUT THE GOSPEL
Titus 2

(LARRY and LOU are sitting and having a discussion.)

LARRY: You know, Lou, I find it fascinating to study different cultures. You can really discover a lot about people around the world by looking at their past and all the things that make them unique.

LOU: You've obviously spent a lot of time at this hobby of yours. So, what's your favourite culture in which part of the world?

LARRY: Well, if you really want me to pick one, I'd have to say it's our own culture here in Canada. It's so diverse and yet we've come together to form a strong country. But the thing that makes me most proud is whenever times are tough, Canadians seem to be at their best. For instance, in World War II, many of the most important Allied victories were directly because of contributions from Canadian soldiers. There are lots of other examples, too.

LOU: It's always good to be proud of our country, but my Mennonite heritage is even more important to me.

LARRY: I know you go to the Mennonite church in town here, but how can you be proud of a group of people that gets together once a week to sit on uncomfortable pews and listen to a boring preacher?

LOU: That shows just how little you know about us. Going to church and being with other believers is an important part of our faith, but there are so many other things as well. We believe very strongly in voluntary service, whether it's helping out with rebuilding after a natural disaster or serving the hungry at the local soup kitchen. But one of the things I'm most proud of is the Mennonite tradition of non-violence. We believe killing people is wrong, no matter what the situation.

LARRY: How in the world can you be proud of something like that? Seems to me you Mennonites are just a bunch of sissies—too scared to stand up and do your share.

LOU: You're entitled to your opinion, but I don't see us that way at all. I think the easiest thing in the world is to respond to violence with more violence. But that just creates a vicious cycle. Where does the violence end? What takes *real* courage is to respond to violence with non-violence and then back it up with a loving attitude. Instead of bombing a developing country that's acting like a bully, we should try to find ways to help them become more prosperous and less violent. It's another way of following the example of Jesus Christ.

LARRY: This is quite an education! I'm not sure I agree with everything you're saying, but it definitely makes me curious to find out more about the Mennonite culture.

LOU: Great! Tell you what, why don't you come to church with me next Sunday. I'll answer as many of your questions as I can and I'll also introduce you to our pastors, they'll be more than happy to talk to you. And if you don't agree with everything you hear, they're always up for a good debate. And besides, their sermons are actually quite interesting.

LARRY: Interesting sermons, I didn't think that was possible. OK, I'll be there. But right now I need to get going and read up all I can find on you Mennonites. Find out a little more about why you're so proud of your traditions.

LOU: Sounds great. See you Sunday.

(They exit.)